LIVING

in

CALM

CONFIDENCE

Register This New Book

Benefits of Registering*

- ✓ FREE **replacements** of lost or damaged books
- ✓ FREE **audiobook** – *Pilgrim's Progress,* audiobook edition
- ✓ FREE information about new titles and other **freebies**

www.anekopress.com/new-book-registration

*See our website for requirements and limitations.

LIVING

in

CALM

CONFIDENCE

The Promise *of* Psalm 16

JOHN KITCHEN

We enjoy hearing from our readers. Please contact us at www.anekopress.com/questions-comments with any questions, comments, or suggestions.

www.jkitchen.org

Living in Calm Confidence

© 2024 by John Kitchen

All rights reserved. Published 2024.

Cover Designer: J. Martin

Cover Image: Adobe Firefly

Editors: Ruth Clark and Jeremiah Zeiset

Aneko Press

www.anekopress.com

Aneko Press, Life Sentence Publishing, and our logos are trademarks of

Life Sentence Publishing, Inc.
203 E. Birch Street
P.O. Box 652
Abbotsford, WI 54405

RELIGION / Christian Living / Inspirational

Paperback ISBN: 979-8-88936-435-1

eBook ISBN: 979-8-88936-436-8

10   9   8   7   6   5   4   3   2   1

Available where books are sold

Dedicated to
Kurds in Christ

CONTENTS

PREFACE

Psalm 16 is a "Jesus-psalm." Jesus said the Psalms speak of him (Luke 24:44), and, as we shall see, this psalm played a pivotal role in Jesus' life and redemptive work. That is reason enough for this book.

In addition, however, I am compelled to write to you because this psalm is changing me. God is using this psalm in life-shaping ways in my life. It is because Psalm 16 is a messianic psalm that it has become so transformative for me. Jesus has met me here and I hope that he will meet you here as well. Through the words of this psalm, Jesus is gifting me with a calm confidence that is not native to my soul.[1] I pray he will give you the same.

---

1   Having already established the theme of Psalm 16 as "Living in Calm Confidence," I was delighted to see that the acclaimed Old Testament commentator C. F. Keil concurred, observing, "There reigns in the whole Psalm, a settled *calm* . . . and a joyous *confidence*, which is certain that everything that it can desire for the present and for the future it possesses in its God" (emphasis added). Keil, C. F., and F. Delitzsch, *Psalms, Commentary on the Old Testament in Ten Volumes* (Grand Rapids: William B. Eerdmans Publishing Company, reprint 1980), 5:217.

I aim, then, to hold out something of what Jesus has given us in this psalm. But I sit down to write this, not knowing if it will ever see the light of day, whether anyone will ever read a single line of it. Why, then, write it at all? If for no other reason, I still write because I have found that the work of Jesus grows fuller in me when I try to set out in letters, words, sentences, and paragraphs what he is teaching me. I have yet to capture its fullness, but the process richens, matures, and helps me savor his work in me through the words of Psalm 16.

So, join me, would you, in considering these life-giving, life-shaping words.

PSALM 16
A Miktam of David.

¹ *Preserve me, O God, for in you I take refuge.*

² *I say to the* LORD, *"You are my Lord; I have no good apart from you."*

³ *As for the saints in the land, they are the excellent ones, in whom is all my delight.*

⁴ *The sorrows of those who run after another god shall multiply; their drink offerings of blood I will not pour out or take their names on my lips.*

⁵ *The* LORD *is my chosen portion and my cup; you hold my lot.*

⁶ *The lines have fallen for me in pleasant places; indeed, I have a beautiful inheritance.*

⁷ *I bless the* LORD *who gives me counsel; in the night also my heart instructs me.*

⁸ *I have set the* LORD *always before me; because he is at my right hand, I shall not be shaken.*

⁹ *Therefore my heart is glad, and my whole being rejoices; my flesh also dwells secure.*

¹⁰ *For you will not abandon my soul to Sheol, or let your holy one see corruption.*

¹¹ *You make known to me the path of life; in your presence there is fullness of joy; at your right hand are pleasures forevermore.*

INTRODUCTION

P salm 16 is designated a *Miktam*. That is a technical term used in the titles to six psalms,[2] all of which are designated *of David*. All are laments, or at least have elements of lament contained in them. And don't you have things over which you are lamenting right now? Four of the six psalms have some notation as to the historical circumstances from which David penned the psalm. And don't you have circumstances that prod you even now toward the Lord?

The precise meaning of *Miktam* is unclear. Some have connected it to a verb meaning "to cover," thus signaling a message of atonement. This may fit the apostle Paul's use of Psalm 16 in Acts 13:35-36. But others see "to cover" as indicating that the psalm holds hidden treasure, valuables to be sought out. Yet others

---

2   Psalm 16, 56, 57, 58, 59, 60.

see in it the meaning "engraving" or "inscription."[3] Still others link it to a word that means "gold," and thus see it as designating "golden truth." But, as Motyer points out, "Why would these psalms as compared to others be termed 'golden' or need emphasis on their permanency?"[4]

What we do know is that Psalm 16 is messianic (you will hear the apostles quote from it in Acts 2:25-28 and 13:35-36). It finds its fulfillment in Jesus and, by way of application, in the lives of those who, by God's grace, live in union with him.

Before diving into the details of the psalm, stand back with me and view its landscape. What lies before us in this psalm? Where are the mountains?

Psalm 16 is messianic

The valleys? The rivers? The meadows? These are metaphorical ways of asking, How is this psalm set before us? Is there an observable structure to this psalm? Are there hints of how the psalmist determined to set out his thoughts?

I perceive a particular kind of arrangement here, a specific form and method by which the author intended to speak to us. Scholars often refer to this pattern as a *chiasm,* or a chiastic arrangement of the material. Don't be put off by the strange word if it is unfamiliar to you. *Chiasm* comes from the Greek letter *chi,* which would roughly be an equivalent to the English letter X. That means the author sets out his material in a pattern that meets in the middle, just as do the two

---

3   Herbert Wolf, "סתם," *Theological Wordbook of the Old Testament* (Chicago: Moody Press, 1980), 1:459.

4   Alec Motyer, *Psalms by the Day* (Fern: Christian Focus Publications, 2016), 40.

axes of the letter X. In a chiasm, the main point is, literally, the central idea, that which lies in the middle. The opening and closing of the psalm run on parallel lines, funneling the reader's attention to the center of the psalm. It begins and ends with similar or corresponding themes. This pattern develops step-by-step, ever narrowing its focus until its key treasure is set out in the middle of the psalm.

This appears to be the case in Psalm 16, with one addition. The chiasm gathers up all of verses 1-10, and then verse 11 serves as a sort of summarizing addendum. The arrangement thus looks like this:

A *¹ Preserve me, O God, for in you I take refuge.*

    B *² I say to the* LORD, *"You are my Lord; I have no good apart from you."*

      ³ As for the saints in the land, they are the excellent ones, in whom is all my delight.

        C *⁴ The sorrows of those who run after another god shall multiply; their drink offerings of blood I will not pour out or take their names on my lips.*

          D *⁵ The* LORD *is my chosen portion and my cup; you hold my lot.*

            ⁶ The lines have fallen for me in pleasant places; indeed, I have a beautiful inheritance.

C *[7] I bless the L*ORD *who gives me counsel; in the night also my heart instructs me.*

B *[8] I have set the L*ORD *always before me; because he is at my right hand, I shall not be shaken.*

[9] Therefore my heart is glad, and my whole being rejoices; my flesh also dwells secure.

A *[10] For you will not abandon my soul to Sheol, or let your holy one see corruption.*

Summary: *[11] You make known to me the path of life; in your presence there is fullness of joy; at your right hand are pleasures forevermore.*

The center of the psalmist's message is found in verses 5 and 6. You will notice that lines C are negative (v. 4) and positive (v. 7) perspectives on the same matter. Negatively stated, the psalmist does not seek counsel from unbelievers or run in their fellowship. Positively stated, he seeks the Lord's counsel and fellowship. Verse 11 serves as a reprise, as if the psalmist (and the one who takes up his words in prayer) pauses to savor the central thought of verses 5 and 6.

Here is the same reality set out in summarized form:

I face death and so flee to God. (v. 1)

   All my hope is in God's immediate presence. (vv. 2-3)

      I will not run with any who diminish God's presence in my life. (v. 4)

         The Lord himself is my treasure and delight. (vv. 5-6)

      I will depend upon God's presence in my life. (v. 7)

   All my hope is in God's immediate presence. (vv. 8-9)

I face death with confidence because of God's promise. (v. 10)

Summary: The path along which God leads me guides me to his presence where his pleasure is realized in me, now and forever. (v. 11)

God promises that the *unfolding of [his] words gives light* (Psalm 119:130). So, in what follows, I attempt to unfold the psalm after this pattern of pairs, leading us then to center our attention on the Lord, who sets himself before us as the only legitimate treasure of his people. As we encounter the Lord, may calm confidence overtake our lives.

PLEA AND PROMISE

Preserve me, O God, for in you I take refuge. (v. 1)

For you will not abandon my soul to Sheol, or let your holy one see corruption. (v. 10)

The life of faith is found in the prayers we raise and the promises on which they are founded. God made the promises. We make our pleas. Our prayers are launched from and rest upon divine promises. Where the two meet, a seed of calming fellowship with God is planted in our hearts.

My brother, if you have a divine promise, you need not plead it with an "if" in it; you may plead with a certainty. If for the mercy which you are now asking, you have God's solemnly pledged word, there will scarce be any room for the caution about submission to his will. You know his will: that will is in the promise; plead it. Do not give him rest until he fulfil it. He meant to fulfil it, or else he would not have given it. God does not give his words merely to quiet our noise, and to keep us hopeful for awhile, with the intention of putting us off at last; but when he speaks, he speaks because he means to act.[5]

—Charles Spurgeon

Chapter 1

PLEA

*Preserve me, O God, for in you I take
refuge.* (v. 1)

D avid's first words are pleadings. He is in trouble;
desperate distress has seized him. He reaches out
urgently for God's intervention.

You are in trouble too, or will be at some point in
your life. David's words have been recorded in Scripture
as God's invitation to make them your own simple plea
in your times of testing and trouble.

Consider the plea we are invited to bring to God.
It is set before us under two banners. The first is a plea
for divine preservation: *Preserve me, O God.*

Clearly, David was in danger. The threat was mor-
tal in nature. Something had to die, and it appeared it

could be him. So he prays. The Hebrew verb means "to keep," "to watch," "to preserve."[6] The root idea is "to exercise great care over"[7] and thus to take care of and to guard. The verb is found again in the assurance that *he who **keeps** you will not slumber. Behold, he who **keeps** Israel will neither slumber nor sleep* (Psalm 121:3-4).

Who doesn't need that? We need God to sit up, take notice, keep watch over us, and exercise himself in our preservation. And this is what God promises to do. You can lay your head on the pillow at night knowing that someone of ultimate strength and infinite love is exercising great care over you. *In peace I will both lie down and sleep; for you alone, O LORD, make me dwell in safety* (Psalm 4:8). Even our hypervigilance is no equal to God's infinite vigilance in caring for us as his own.

How do I get in on that?

The second banner is a plea to find *refuge* in God: *Preserve me, O God, for in you I take refuge* (Psalm 16:1).

Note that little word *for*. It introduces the ground upon which David believes God will *preserve* him. The cry, *Preserve me* is the only request in the entire psalm. It has just left David's lips. Though facing danger and death, he asks for only one thing. David spends the rest of the psalm celebrating God and his grace.

Why could David have confidence that God would *preserve* him? How could Jesus have that confidence when he took up this psalm and made it his own? How can you?

---

6   Brown, Francis, S. R. Driver, and Charles A. Briggs, *A Hebrew and English Lexicon of the Old Testament* (Oxford: Clarendon Press, 1906), 1036.

7   John Hartley, "רָמַשׁ," *Theological Wordbook of the Old Testament* by Harris, R. Laird, Gleason L. Archer Jr., and Bruce K. Waltke (Chicago: Moody Press, 1980), 2:939.

Simply and only because *in you I take refuge.*

The word translated *refuge* is used in the Old Testament of a bird finding shelter,[8] of taking refuge in a cave,[9] of taking shelter from a rainstorm,[10] and of finding safety behind a shield.[11]

To have the plea come to pass (God preserving us), we must take refuge in God. If you don't take refuge in God, you can't expect him to save you.

So I must ask, Have you run to the Lord for refuge?

I am not asking if you have called on God to bail you out of the mess you are in. I am not inquiring whether you have thrown up a prayer to heaven, thinking, "What could it hurt? Might as well, just in case!" I am asking whether your practice (taking refuge in God) matches your plea (for him to save you).

Have you run to the Lord for refuge?

The safety of an elevated branch does the vulnerable bird little good unless he takes flight and plants his feet upon it. The safety of the cave yields no relief to the defenseless one who gazes on it from across the valley. The hiker is soaked to the skin in a rainstorm if he only pictures a roof over his head and never seeks it out. A shield at one's side does no good unless, in faith, it is lifted against the onslaught of the enemy.

You can't just mail in your request to God. You must position yourself in faith before the Lord as you lift up to him your plea for preservation.

---

8   Psalm 57:1; 61:4; 91:4.

9   Deuteronomy 32:37.

10   Isaiah 4:6; 25:4; Job 24:8.

11   Psalm 144:2.

How do I take refuge in the Lord? David himself will tell us with his next pen stroke (v. 2). But let us not get ahead of ourselves.

Chapter 2

PROMISE

For you will not abandon my soul to Sheol,
or let your holy one see corruption. (v. 10)

You are in trouble. You need God to intervene – to sit up, take notice, and act to *preserve* and save you (v. 1). What confidence or assurance do you have that God will do so? God's own promise!

God speaks with the backing of his own unfailing, eternal faithfulness, promising us life and assuring us that death will not have the final word over us. God spoke all things into being. He invited us to share all things in joyful fellowship with him. His singular restriction came with a warning of death. When our parents chose independence, the warned-of death became reality. If God is life and if all life comes from him, and he

7

hands it out one breath at a time to us, then what must independence from him be, if not death? But God, in the face of our parents' rebellion, promised to reverse that curse and give us life again. A promised deliverer would come, stand in our place, bear our curse, remove our sin, and assuage God's wrath. And he would rise again, unable to ever die again. This very life of God's deliverer would be given to us.

This was David's great hope. How much of this detail he understood we do not know, but he spoke of the coming, risen, triumphant deliverer and his triumph over death, saying, *For you will not abandon my soul to Sheol, or let your holy one see corruption* (v. 10).

The whole of this psalm, written by David, was ultimately fulfilled in his greater Son, the Messiah, the Lord Jesus Christ.

That is how the apostles understood this psalm. Consider how the New Testament writers use Psalm 16. On the day of Pentecost the apostle Peter applied Psalm 16:8-11 to Jesus: *"Men of Israel, hear these words: Jesus of Nazareth, a man attested to you by God with mighty works and wonders and signs that God did through him in your midst, as you yourselves know— this Jesus, delivered up according to the definite plan and foreknowledge of God, you crucified and killed by the hands of lawless men. God raised him up, loosing the pangs of death, because it was not possible for him to be held by it"* (Acts 2:22-24).

Then Peter applied Psalm 16:8-11 to Jesus, saying, *For David says concerning him, "'I saw the Lord always before me, for he is at my right hand that I may not be shaken; therefore my heart was glad, and my tongue rejoiced; my flesh also will dwell in hope. For you will not abandon my soul to Hades, or let your Holy One see corruption. You have made known to me the paths of life; you will make me full of gladness with your presence"* (Acts 2:25-28).

Peter applied the promise of Psalm 16:10 to Jesus' resurrection from the dead. This guarantee from God created an impossibility: that death might hold Jesus. Not just unlikely. Not just improbable. Impossible.

What is the basis of this impossibility? Was it Jesus' own inherent existence as life itself (John 14:6)? Was it his designation as *the resurrection and the life* (John 11:25)? These obviously have a powerful part to play in the reality of resurrection life in Jesus, but neither one is the basis upon which Peter declares

It was impossible for death to hold Jesus.

this impossibility. It was impossible for death to hold Jesus, *For* [this declares the grounds of the impossibility] *David says concerning him* (Acts 2:25). The promise of God handcuffs death! Death loses all power in the presence of God's promise. Death is stripped of its possibilities by a word from God!

All this psalm describes was designed most fundamentally for the person of Jesus Christ. It then also assures this triumph, by relationship to Jesus, for all those who are "in Christ."

"Brothers, I may say to you with confidence about the patriarch David that he both died

> *and was buried, and his tomb is with us*
> *to this day. Being therefore a prophet, and*
> *knowing that God had sworn with an oath*
> *to him that he would set one of his descen-*
> *dants on his throne, he foresaw and spoke*
> *about the resurrection of the Christ, that he*
> *was not abandoned to Hades, nor did his*
> *flesh see corruption. This Jesus God raised*
> *up, and of that we all are witnesses. Being*
> *therefore exalted at the right hand of God,*
> *and having received from the Father the*
> *promise of the Holy Spirit, he has poured*
> *out this that you yourselves are seeing and*
> *hearing.*" (Acts 2:29-33)

This resurrection life is ours now through the indwell-ing life of Jesus made real in us through the Holy Spirit inhabiting us. This life is ours forever because Jesus rose from the dead. Though physical death may come to us, eternal and spiritual death never will. *But in fact Christ has been raised from the dead, the firstfruits of those who have fallen asleep. But each in his own order: Christ the firstfruits, then at his coming those who belong to Christ* (1 Corinthians 15:20, 23).

Similarly, while preaching in Antioch, Paul applied the promise of verse 10 to Jesus.

> "*And as for the fact that he raised him from*
> *the dead, no more to return to corrup-*
> *tion, he has spoken in this way, 'I will give*
> *you the holy and sure blessings of David.'*

Therefore he says also in another psalm, 'You will not let your Holy One see corruption.' For David, after he had served the purpose of God in his own generation, fell asleep and was laid with his fathers and saw corruption, but he whom God raised up did not see corruption. Let it be known to you therefore, brothers, that through this man forgiveness of sins is proclaimed to you, and by him everyone who believes is freed from everything from which you could not be freed by the law of Moses."
(Acts 13:34-39)

The first promise cited (v. 34) came through Isaiah (Isaiah 55:3). The second comes straight out of Psalm 16:10. Unless Christ first returns, you and I will, like David, die. We will *"[fall] asleep and . . . [see] corruption"* (Acts 13:36). But when Christ does return, we will have life. The promise of God guarantees it. It is impossible for it to turn out any other way.

The question is, Do you and I, like David, *[serve] the purpose of God in [our] own generation* (v. 36)? Do you know what God's purpose is? Do you know what his intention is for you within his larger plan? His purpose is greater than your urge to stay alive and to be comfortable while alive. Will you fulfill that purpose in reliance on his indwelling life? Will you fulfill it even unto physical death, knowing that on the other side of that brief stab of pain is eternal, uninterrupted, unconquerable life?

The Old Testament again and again speaks the promise of resurrection and the eternal life to follow.[12] But what is the real value of a promise, particularly when you are staring down death?

> *For the Son of God, Jesus Christ, . . . was*
> *not Yes and No, but in him it is always Yes.*
> *For all the promises of God find their Yes*
> *in him. That is why it is through him that*
> *we utter our Amen to God for his glory.*
> (2 Corinthians 1:19-20)

In sending his Son, God removed "No" from his relationship with all who are sanctified in him. In sending Jesus, the Father threw open the Scriptures and shouted "Yes!" to every promise he ever made to us. Jesus means the end of "No" from the Father. Through Jesus, the Father has preapproved the full delivery of every one of his promises to anyone who will come to him through his Son.

Find a promise from God in the Bible. Know that the Father has already said "Yes!" to any prayer you rightly raise to ask for its fulfillment in your life. His "Yes!" applies to the fulfillment of that promise in your life, not necessarily to your timing or the imagined way it must be fulfilled. Leave that to him, for he is wiser than you are and more predisposed to generosity and faithfulness than you can imagine.

In view of the hard reality of our need, but also in perceiving the superior nature of the promise and the

---

12   Job 19:25-27; Psalm 17:15; 49:15; 73:23-28; Isaiah 25:8; 26:19; 53:10; Ezekiel 37:1-14; Daniel 12:2-3; Hosea 13:14.

Promiser who stands behind it, we look at the promises of God and add our amen.

Through overuse, we may become numb to the meaning of that simple word. It means something like "Yes!" or "Let it be so!" We turn to God. We find him holding out his promises to us in Christ and saying, "Yes! Yes! This is yours! Take it! I want you to have it!" We, then, in faith, respond, "Yes! Let it be so in my life!"

"Yes! Let it be so in my life!"

The risen, victorious, reigning Lord Jesus Christ bears the title *the Amen* (Revelation 3:14). He is God's "Yes!" In Jesus, the Father is declaring over every promise he has ever made, "Let it be so!"

Your amen echoes God's amen, and his will comes about in your experience. When your amen meets God's "Yes!" you get grace, and God gets glory.

See in this light that your plea is not a helpless whimper, made as you go down for the third time. Your plea is planted squarely on God's promise and is thus as much a declaration of faith as it is a cry of desperation.

In this way we will come, in this life and the next, to testify, as did Joshua, *Not one word of all the good promises that the Lord had made . . . had failed; all came to pass* (Joshua 21:45). Solomon, David's son and successor, could stand over his father's grave, holding his father's psalm, and declare, *"Blessed be the Lord who has given . . . according to all that he promised"* (1 Kings 8:56).

You and I can walk in an even *better hope* (Hebrews 7:19), calling upon God through his risen Son, knowing that *faithful is He who calls you, and He also will bring it to pass* (1 Thessalonians 5:24 NASB).

CONSECRATION AND CONFIDENCE

I say to the LORD, "You are my Lord; I have no good apart from you." As for the saints in the land, they are the excellent ones, in whom is all my delight. (vv. 2-3)

I have set the LORD always before me; because he is at my right hand, I shall not be shaken. Therefore my heart is glad, and my whole being rejoices; my flesh also dwells secure. (vv. 8-9)

A plea (v. 1) launched to God's throne from the foundation of a divine promise (v. 10) births assurance in the one praying. The promise woos us into fixing our hope singularly on the Promiser. The one praying is fixed exclusively on the one making the promise. This consecration to God (v. 2), in time and with experience, also becomes a consecration to God's people (v. 3). Somewhere in that unfolding fellowship with God and his people, an unshakeable confidence begins to grow (vv. 8-9).

> "The root of all steadfastness is consecration to God."[13]
> —Alexander MacLaren

> "I claim no right to myself, no right to this understanding, this will, these affections that are in me. Neither do I have any right to this body or its members, no right to this tongue, to these hands, feet, ears or eyes. I have given myself clear away and not retained anything of my own."[14]
> —Jonathan Edwards

13 Douglas, Charles Noel, comp., *Forty Thousand Quotations: Prose and Poetical* (New York: Halcyon House, 1917). *www.bartleby.com/lit-hub/forty-thousand-quotations-prose-and-poetical/*.

14 MacArthur, John F. Jr., *Matthew, Vol. 2, MacArthur New Testament Commentary* (Chicago: Moody Press, 1985), 215.

Chapter 3

CONSECRATION TO GOD

*I say to the LORD, "You are my Lord; I have
no good apart from you."* (v. 2)

H ere we have our answer to the question of how
one takes refuge in the Lord (v. 1), who alone is
life (v. 10). Consecration is the key to security, refuge,
and safety in Christ. The word *consecration* is not found
in verse 2, but it is what David describes.

Notice the quotation marks, marking off what David
says to God. *I say to the LORD, "You are my Lord."* David
addressed *the LORD.* The English used here represents
the personal name of God, often transliterated into
English as *Yahweh.* This is not a title by which God
is designated, such as God Almighty or the Most
High. This, rather, is God's personal name. As such it

designates and sets out God's character. It is not descriptive merely of his abilities or actions. It also designates him as the covenant-making, covenant-keeping God. *Yahweh* pursues us, seeks us out, and establishes his covenant with us. He does this by taking upon himself the obligation of both forming and keeping the covenant. He simply invites us into relationship with himself. He, of course, ultimately stood among us in Jesus Christ, God in flesh, who *"came to seek and to save the lost"* (Luke 19:10).

Addressing *Yahweh,* David declares to him, *"You are my Lord."* Here David uses the Hebrew word *Adonai.* In shorthand, *Adonai* designates one's master, one's owner. In naming someone *Adonai,* you confess that he is over you and justly rules you. *Adonai* has authority over us. In taking up the word, we confess that *Yahweh* has the right to our absolute submission and obedience.

In David's sentence, *"You are my Lord,"* the emphasis lies upon the pronoun *my.* David is not merely parroting good theology. This is more than a pious form for prayer-making. This is personal.

One who prays in this way is confessing before God, "In view of your great redemptive love that sought and bought me for yourself, I gladly bow my entire life to you. I am glad to live under your rule and authority and to curb my life to fulfill your mission and to build your kingdom." To pray thus is to say to the great lover of my soul, "You are my Owner, Master, and Sovereign."

Not long ago, I was meeting with a young man who had come to faith in Jesus. I was preparing him for baptism. He was troubled, however. He recounted his delight at discovering the beauty of God as loving, seeking, and redeeming. Compared to the local religion in which he had been raised, this was remarkable and joyous to him. Yet he wondered aloud to me, "But why does the New Testament talk about Jesus' followers being slaves?"

My new brother needed to discover that being Jesus' slave does not stand in contrast to being the object of his love. In fact, our willing slavery is the product of that sacrificial love. It is a servitude not enforced by mere power and demand, but secured by the bonds of love and grace. Once in the grip of that grace, one locks the shackles of submission around one's own wrists. For the confession of absolute consecration knows, *"I have no good apart from you."*

All that is good in my life begins and ends with the Lord.

The expression is difficult to translate into English.[15] Perhaps the best we can do is a literal rendering: "my good – not beyond you." But what does that mean?

The key seems to lie in our understanding of the preposition rendered *apart from* or *beyond*. It has a breadth of meaning, but here it seems to express excess and may designate something that "does not lie outside" the Lord.[16] David has discovered that there is nothing truly *good* to be found outside of his fellowship with the Lord.

---

15   Indeed, the translators of the LXX (the Septuagint) went in a different direction than the Hebrew, opting for τῶν ἀγαθῶν μου οὐ χρείαν ἔχεις (15:2), *you have no need for my good.*

16   Brown, Driver, and Briggs, *A Hebrew and English Lexicon of the Old Testament,* 755.

All that is good in my life begins and ends with the Lord. All good not only comes from him (James 1:17), but it also can only be enjoyed in fellowship with him. All that is good in my life comes to a halt if I depart from him. The greatest good that could ever come to me is not beyond his ability and cannot be fully enjoyed apart from him.

As you can see, *"I have no good apart from you"* is a loaded statement. It is shorthand for praying this:

> "All that is good in my life comes from you, and there is no limit to the good you can pour into my life. So ultimately, 'good' is not something you give to me, but who you are to me. Lord, you are my good. And anything and everything I might experience outside of my relationship with you ceases to be good. All the good stuff the world offers is like garbage if I can't enjoy it in relationship with you. All the sweet things the world offers are like gravel in my mouth if I can't enjoy them in relationship with you. The best of this world means nothing to me if I can't enjoy it with you. God, you are my good, and all else is good only as I experience it in relationship with you. Ice cream ceases to be sweet if I eat it out of fellowship with you. Even sex isn't satisfying and life-giving if I engage in it outside of your will. The creation loses its luster if I don't view it in fellowship with you. Work is distasteful if I don't undertake

it with you and for you. Truly, Lord, I have
no good apart from you!"

Another psalmist admitted as much when he prayed,
There is nothing on earth I desire besides you (Psalm 73:25).
When you have the Lord, you have it all. When you
forsake the Lord, you forfeit all else. C. S. Lewis was
right when he said, "He who has God and everything
else has no more than he who has God alone."[17]

The calm confidence we need, as with every other
good, will only be found in the intimacy of complete
consecration to our Master.

---

17   C. S. Lewis, *The Weight of Glory and Other Addresses* (New York:
HarperOne, 2001), 34.

Chapter 4

CONSECRATION TO GOD'S PEOPLE

As for the saints in the land, they are the excellent ones, in whom is all my delight. (v. 3)

When you consecrate yourself to God alone (v. 2), you discover that God is not alone. He has a family (v. 3). To relate to him is to relate to them. And how you relate to them is a major indicator of how you truly relate to him. Like the rest of us, John discovered this the hard way: *Whoever loves God must also love his brother* (1 John 4:21).

But the Lord doesn't intend this as a grudging duty – akin to your childhood best friend bringing his annoying little brother along on your long-planned

23

day together because his mom made him. No, once we discover there is no good to be had outside of fellowship with God (v. 2), there grows an awareness that our fellowship with God is enjoyed most intensely when we are embedded in relationship with his people (v. 3). My greatest good is to be found in relationship, not isolation. My welfare is tied to my connection not only with God, but also to my relationship with others of like faith and heart.

We find here a progression in how David refers to the people of God. They are holy (*saints*), noble (*the excellent ones*), and delightful (*my delight*). Consider each step along this progression of appreciation.

God's people are designated as *the saints,* or, *the holy ones.* As such, they are not merely formally religious people. The root word is used of God himself and then also of those consecrated to him in faith and obedience. They are the

God is enjoyed most intensely when we are embedded in relationship with his people.

ones that the *holy one* (v. 10) declared to be *the holy ones* (v. 3 NRSV) by his grace. It is used of priests (including Aaron himself), Levites, prophets, and Nazarites. Within the context of the psalm, it specifically designates those who, like you, *take refuge* in the Lord (v. 1) and *say to the* Lord, *"You are my Lord"* (v. 2), and who have also come to confess to him: *"I have no good apart from you"* (v. 2). These are the people you discover along the path in your spiritual journey, pilgrims of the heart, who also know the Lord by covenant, have submitted to him as Master (v. 1), and who find all of life only in relationship to him (v. 2).

These fellow travelers stand by grace as *the saints*. But they become more to us than their title. Our shared journey with them proves them to be *the excellent ones*. Experience with them teaches me to say of them what God says of them. The basic connotation of the word describes that which is wide or broad (on a horizontal plane) or lofty (on a vertical plane). It is used to describe the waters of the sea, a ship sailing upon them, a flourishing tree or vine upon the earth. It is used figuratively of kings, nations, and even gods. It is applied to nobles, chieftains, and priests.[18] Such are not to be found among the majority. They are a select division among the religious crowd. They prove themselves exceptional in the "long obedience in the same direction."[19] I strive to be one among them. It is my honor to walk beside them. I treasure and prioritize my relationship with them – other blessed travelers of *the Way*.[20]

Indeed, journeying together, they have become *my delight*. Their company pleases me. They consistently (though not always) create delight in my inner person. I cherish time and relationship with them. I prioritize opportunities to be with them. Am I comfortable with this notion that a shared pleasure is a multiplied pleasure?

---

18 Brown, Driver, and Briggs, *A Hebrew and English Lexicon of the Old Testament*, 12.

19 Eugene Peterson, *A Long Obedience in the Same Direction* (Downers Grove, Illinois: InterVarsity Press, 2021).

20 Acts 9:2; 19:9, 23; 24:14, 22.

Perhaps it is not comfortable, but I am enlarged by it. And this, I am finding, is *good* (v. 2).

So, there is, experientially, a progression in our relationship with other Yahweh-seekers: the formality of living under a common covenant (*the saints*), the discovery of their heart as *the excellent ones,* and the personal pleasure of their company (*my delight*).

This latter discovery returns me to the *good* I have found in God alone (v. 2). Oddly, having been guided to God alone, I find my highest *good* (or stature, completeness, and pleasure) in fellowship with like-minded people of God. In their midst, with God dwelling among us, I find my greatest joy, explore my constantly being-redeemed nature, and become what God wants to make of me.

Paradoxically, my life alone with God is best discovered while living among other solitary beings, sold out singularly to him as their highest and only *good.* This is a beautiful glimpse of what comes to full expression in the New Testament church of Jesus Christ. Over sixty times in the New Testament we believers are called saints, those made so by God's grace through Jesus. In its pages we discover the church as a new humanity, a new community, a new people, a new nation. Where people found new life through Jesus, they began gathering for worship, prayer, teaching, fellowship, support, and relationship. That is to say, they found that *the saints* truly are *the excellent ones.* And, given time and experience, they became *my delight.*

But if Psalm 16 genuinely was Jesus' prayer, who were *the saints* and *the excellent ones* of his day? The religious leaders and those who followed them were the very ones who crucified him. Were *the saints* and *the excellent ones* to be found in Jesus' disciples? Even they disowned and abandoned him.

I think the answer is both yes and no. Yes, they were found in the disciples, but not merely the eleven. It also included those who made up the larger body of the faithful. Perhaps they were to be found among the 120 in the upper room after his resurrection (Acts 1:15). Peter was among them. So, they are not

> *Jesus was forsaken so you never will be.*

perfectly faithful people, but they are those who, even when unfaithful, are ever returning to Jesus and the path of following him. Humble people. Those who own their sins and failures. Individuals, utterly dependent upon Jesus and his Spirit. Those who always return to and are determined to continue on *the Way.*

That's the yes. But there is also the no. In the end, Jesus was utterly alone, even crying to the Father, *"Why have you forsaken me?"* (Psalm 22:1; Matthew 27:46). Jesus was forsaken precisely so he could promise us, *"I will never leave you nor forsake you"* (Hebrews 13:5).

Paul, in his final written communication before martyrdom, testified, *All . . . turned away from me* (2 Timothy 1:15), and *no one came to stand by me, but all deserted me* (2 Timothy 4:16). Yet, he also testified, *The Lord stood by me* (2 Timothy 4:17). And, truth be told, beyond the emotional failure of *all* those he had counted on, there were joyful, faithful exceptions (2 Timothy 1:16-18; 4:11).

Jesus was forsaken so you never will be. And he has set you in company with the others to whom he has made this covenant promise. Some of them will fail you. That will hurt more than words can describe. But others, as living emblems of their Savior, will stand by you in your worst hours, even your final hour. You will discover that they are *the excellent ones,* the ones in whom the Lord allows you to discover exceptional *delight.*

Chapter 5

CONFIDENCE OF SECURITY

I have set the LORD always before me;
because he is at my right hand, I shall not
be shaken. (v. 8)

O ur orientation toward the material world leads us to say that a person can't be in two places at the same time. This spatial orientation makes it difficult to get our minds around the next two lines of David's prayer. The Lord is depicted as being both *before me* and *at my right hand.* How am I to understand this?

How do I *set the LORD always before me?*

The verb rendered *set* is intensive.[21] There has been a

---

21 "Psalm 16:8 is a familiar verse to many Jewish people today. Most Jewish homes have a *Sheviti* plaque on a wall. *Sheviti* means 'I have set.'" William Varner, *Awake O Harp: A Devotional Commentary on the Psalms* (The Woodlands: Kress Biblical Resources, 2011), 45.

determination; a decisive choice has been made. There is a *set* of the mind and will. Yes, the Lord is omnipresent, fully present in the fullness of his divine being at every point in reality. So, to say that I have set him *before* me is another way of saying I have determined to look upon no other. I have decided to fix my eyes on the Lord instead of on the myriad matters of life that call for my attention. I have adopted, to echo one of the films in the *Rocky* series, "the eye of the tiger." I will not break the gaze of my attention, thoughts, and heart upon the Lord – who he is, what he has done, and what he has promised yet to do. We are called to run the race of this life, *fixing our eyes on Jesus* (Hebrews 12:2 NASB).

> *I have decided to fix my eyes on the Lord.*

How do I do that? Just what David has been saying in Psalm 16:5-7 – by treasuring the Lord and his immediate presence in my life as the greatest gift I've ever received or will ever receive; by living life in an active, continual flow of fellowship with him; and by taking in his Word, gaining counsel from it for each event of each day, even to the point of filling my mind and heart with it in the idle moments of life.[22]

Only when you have *set the LORD always before* you can you say with confidence, *He is at my right hand.*

Many people complain, "Where was the Lord when I needed him?" even though they haven't been setting him continually before themselves.

---

22   Cf. the use of the same Hebrew verb in Psalm 119:30: *I set your rules before me.*

What does it mean to have the Lord *at [your] right hand*?

The right hand is a place of *authority and power.* When Jesus had conquered all his foes, *he sat down at the right hand of God* (Hebrews 10:12). There, *at the right hand of God [he sits], with angels, authorities, and powers having been subjected to him* (1 Peter 3:22). He is there for his people. The Father *worked in Christ when he raised him from the dead and seated him at his right hand in the heavenly places, far above all rule and authority and power and dominion, and above every name that is named, not only in this age but also in the one to come. And he put all things under his feet and gave him as head over all things to the church, which is his body, the fullness of him who fills all in all* (Ephesians 1:20-23).

If you've been praying with David, you have already rejoiced in the Lord's supremacy, confessing *to the Lord, "You are my Lord"* (Psalm 16:2). You have the one of ultimate authority and power standing in authority and power over your life.

The right hand is a place of *honor and dignity.* This is precisely why the writer to the Hebrews asked, *To which of the angels has he ever said, "Sit at my right hand"?* (Hebrews 1:13). The *right hand* of God is set apart for the Son of God, not created beings. When the mother of James and John petitioned Jesus, *"Say that these two sons of mine are to sit, one at your right hand and one at your left, in your kingdom"* (Matthew 20:21), she was trying to get her sons honored positions ahead of the other disciples. Had Jesus granted her request, however, it would not have been long before James and John fought over who got positioned at Jesus' right hand.

If you've been praying along with David, you have already exalted the Lord to the preeminent place in your life. You have declared, *"I have no good apart from you."*

The right hand is an *unprotected place.* Roughly 90 percent of the human population is right-handed. In a battle, most would have their sword in their right hand and their shield in their left. This would render them less protected on the right side. But that is precisely where the Lord is![23]

Asaph went through a crisis of faith (Psalm 73:2-22). He admits, *My feet had almost stumbled* (v. 2). He felt that everything about his life of faith and obedience had been *all in vain* (v. 13). But when he positioned his heart again before the Lord in worship (v. 17), his eyes were opened to what had been true all along. At every step of the crisis, the Lord had kept him near. He awakened from his stupor only to discover that *you hold my right hand* (v. 23). Even while he contemplated tossing in the towel spiritually, while he nearly gave way to temptation, the Lord was holding his right hand. In his most vulnerable state, Asaph's right hand was cradled in the omnipotently powerful *right hand of God* (cf. Psalm 18:35; 44:3; 63:8; 121:5; 138:7; 139:10).

As it was for David and Asaph, so it is for you. *I, the LORD your God, hold your right hand; it is I who say to you, "Fear not, I am the one who helps you"* (Isaiah 41:13). The one who lives with the Lord at his *right hand* can

---

23   Allen P. Ross, *A Commentary on the Psalms, Volume 1 (1-41)* (Grand Rapids: Kregel Academic, 2012), 408.

look forward to one day enjoying the pleasures that await at his *right hand* (Psalm 16:11).

Only with the Lord set before you and with him firmly at your right hand can you pray, *I shall not be shaken.* This is not a voucher for a trouble-free existence; rather, it is the confidence that, when misfortune comes, you won't be overthrown by it. When trouble arrives, the one with the Lord before him and beside him faces it with the confidence that he will not thereby be ultimately defeated or toppled from his relationship with God.

Chapter 6

CONFIDENCE OF SAFETY

*Therefore my heart is glad, and my whole being
rejoices; my flesh also dwells secure.* (v. 9)

Spiritual confidence is, at one level, a matter of simple
logic. The confidence held forth at the end of verse
8 is now enlarged upon. *Therefore* signals that the confidence held forth there and expanded upon here flows
logically out of what has come before – the Lord before
and beside me. Verse 9 opens with an expression that
means "according to such conditions" or "that being
so."[24] With the Lord set before me and filling the hori-
zon of my every thought about, and calculation of, my
life in this world, and with him faithfully stationed at

---

24   A combination of the preposition ל and the adverbial particle כֵּן.
      Brown, Driver, and Briggs, *A Hebrew and English Lexicon of the Old
      Testament*, 486.

my right hand, guiding me personally along the path, I come into a certain God-confidence.

In that arrangement, I am transformed at three different levels of my being: *my heart, my whole being,* and *my flesh.*

One's *heart* is one's core, the place from which thoughts, emotions, and choices are weighed, chosen, and sent forth. It should be guarded above all else, for from it flows all the rest of one's life and its circumstances (Proverbs 4:23).

The expression *my whole being* is more literally, *my glory.*[25] Strange as it may sound to our ears, there are a few places in the Old Testament where *glory* may better be taken as a reference to the liver.[26] The context here in Psalm 16, after all, does mention other body parts: *my heart* (vv. 7, 9), *my right hand* (v. 8), *my flesh* (v. 9). The liver can be spoken of metaphorically, much as we do the heart. Just like with *heart, liver* would not be considered literally in this case, but as the core and center of oneself. It is a poetic way of designating "the seat of honour in the inner man, the noblest part of man."[27] There is no more precious place than this.

But it is not only the deepest, immaterial part of me that God redeems, it is also the whole of me. God also redeems *my flesh. "God is spirit, and those who worship him must worship in spirit and truth"* (John 4:24). Our

---

25 The LXX went a different direction altogether, rendering it ἡ γλῶσσά μου, *my tongue.*

26 The two are different by only one letter: *glory* (kābôd) and *liver* (kābēd). Cf. John N. Oswalt, "דבֵָּכ," *Theological Wordbook of the Old Testament* (Chicago: Moody Press, 1980), 1:427.

27 Brown, Driver, and Briggs, *A Hebrew and English Lexicon of the Old Testament,* 458.

worship of God is, therefore, not a matter of geography (vv. 20-21), but of spiritual transformation (v. 23). God redeems us from the inside out. But let us be clear, that that does include the outside of us – not only our spirit and soul, but also our bodies. God redeems *my flesh.*

This is precisely what Jesus secured for us through his bodily resurrection from the dead. This is why Peter, on the day of Pentecost, preached the risen Jesus using Psalm 16:8-11 as his text (Acts 2:25-28). We can live in confidence, even in the face of death, nay, *especially* in the face of death. The last enemy has been conquered (1 Corinthians 15:26). Jesus rightly exhorts us, *"Fear not."* And this is because Jesus can announce, *"I am . . . the living one. I died, and behold I am alive forevermore, and I have the keys of Death and Hades"* (Revelation 1:17-18).

The last enemy has been conquered.

At Jesus' return *the dead in Christ will rise* (1 Thessalonians 4:16).

> *We shall all be changed, in a moment, in the twinkling of an eye, at the last trumpet. For the trumpet will sound, and the dead will be raised imperishable, and we shall be changed. For this perishable body must put on the imperishable, and this mortal body must put on immortality. When the perishable puts on the imperishable, and the mortal puts on immortality, then shall come to pass the saying that is written: "Death is swallowed up in victory." "O death, where is*

your victory? O death, where is your sting?"
(1 Corinthians 15:51-55).

When the Father raised his Son from the grave in *the power of an indestructible life* (Hebrews 7:16), he set in motion events that cannot fail to come to pass. The promise of God, secured by the death and resurrection of his Son, is assured. My *inner* person (*my heart*), my *whole* person (*my whole being*), and my *physical* person (*my flesh*) are all redeemed by Christ!

Such security emanates through one's entire being, causing three realities to erupt from within us. What shall not befall me because of the Lord being before and beside me (*I shall not be shaken,* Psalm 16:8) is now stated positively as what shall happen within me.

My spirit *is glad.* My entire being *rejoices.* The two Hebrew verbs are roughly synonymous. Shockwaves of gladness run through every stratum of the one who rests in the redemption of Jesus. In *my heart,* I think joy, emote with joy, and choose from the midst of joy. From my entire being joy springs forth. No part of me is untouched by its overflowing fountain. My greatest good is found in making much of him who has made me the object of his grace.

In addition, my flesh *dwells secure.* In this world, *my flesh* faces many threats – sickness and disease, accident and tragedy, attack and hatred. Yet, it *dwells secure.* The verb, at its root, has the meaning of "trust." Security rests trustingly on the promise of another. At times, it is found in combination with a verb meaning "quietness" (Isaiah 30:15; 32:17). While joy erupts from within us, finding its way out in both vocal and physical expression, the security of God's promise brings a quiet confidence to every cell of our body. All the energy released in acclamations of joyful praise comes from the quiet confidence of being held firmly in the grip of a divine faithfulness that cannot fail.

When Jesus' lifeless body was placed in Joseph's tomb, it was *secure,* wrapped in the surety of the promise of the God who cannot lie. When the time comes to close your eyes for the last time, you enjoy even greater confidence and security, for in Jesus the promise has been secured; he is the prototype of all who will be raised to life at his return. In Jesus, the promise of your resurrection is *Yes* and *Amen* (2 Corinthians 1:20).

Joy, of course, is not the same as happiness. Both are positive, pleasurable, and desirable, but they are not identical. Happiness is circumstantial, while joy is foundational. Happiness grows out of what happens to us, while joy endures no matter what happens to us. Happiness is momentary, while joy is enduring. Happiness is founded on pleasure, while joy arises from principle.

> *In Jesus, the promise of your resurrection is "Yes" and "Amen."*

Joy is not what you feel, but what and who you know. Joy is not what happens to you, but how you see what happens to you. Joy is not what you think, but what you are convinced of. Joy is not something worked up, but something that bubbles up. Joy is not determined by your circumstances, but by your convictions. Joy is not something to obtain, but a flow of life entered.

The workers in Nehemiah's day were reminded that *"the joy of the LORD is your strength"* (Nehemiah 8:10). Joy begets strength. If you reduce the joy, you reduce the strength. If you increase joy, you increase strength. This, however, does not work in the other direction. Increased strength does not bring about increased joy.

I have joy precisely because (*For,* Psalm 16:10) God has promised not to abandon his Son (and all who are by God's grace brought into union with him) to death (v. 10)!

SEPARATION AND SUFFICIENCY

*The sorrows of those who run after another
god shall multiply; their drink offerings
of blood I will not pour out or take their
names on my lips.* (v. 4)

*I bless the Lord who gives me counsel; in
the night also my heart instructs me.* (v. 7)

Exclusive consecration to the Lord (vv. 2-3) is the soil
from which a growing confidence in his providential
rule of my life springs forth (vv. 8-9). This further
results in both separation from other options (v. 4) and
confidence in the sufficiency of the Lord (v. 7).

"Those that multiply gods multiply griefs
to themselves; for, whoever thinks one God
too little, will find two too many, and yet
hundreds not enough."[28]
—Matthew Henry

The Holy Ghost wrote the Word, and if
you make much of the Word, He will make
much of you. It is through the Word that
He reveals Himself. Between those covers
is a living Book. God wrote it and it is still
vital and effective and alive. God is in this
Book, the Holy Ghost is in this Book, and if
you want to find Him, go into this Book."[29]
—A.W. Tozer

28 Matthew Henry, *Matthew Henry's Commentary on the Whole Bible:
    Complete and Unabridged* (Peabody, Mass.: Hendrickson Publishers,
    Inc., 1991), 763.
29 A.W. Tozer, *The Tozer Pulpit*, volume 2, comp. Gerald B. Smith
    (Harrisburg, Pennsylvania: Christian Publications, 1968), 116-117.

Chapter 7

SEPARATION

The sorrows of those who run after another
god shall multiply; their drink offerings
of blood I will not pour out or take their
names on my lips. (v. 4)

Consecration to God (v. 2) and to his people (v. 3), by definition, requires a step back from those who do not trust and honor him (v. 4). It is inevitable. Unavoidable, really. When you pass into your home, you cease to be outside of the home. To dive into the pool is to cease to be out of the pool. The one eliminates the other.

So too, as David, along with others, cries to God alone (vv. 1-3), he is thereby stepping out of the fellowship of those who do not so run to God (v. 4). This is not a call for isolation. As the apostle clarified, *I wrote to you in my letter not to associate with sexually immoral people—not at all meaning the sexually immoral of this world, or the greedy and swindlers, or idolaters, since then you would need to go out of the world* (1 Corinthians 5:9-10).

This is a simple acknowledgement of the facts. *What portion does a believer share with an unbeliever?* (2 Corinthians 6:15). There is only one answer. *What agreement has the temple of God with idols?* (v. 16). Again, the answer may be distasteful to our current cultural palate, but it is not difficult.

Why? Because *we are the temple of the living God; as God said, "I will make my dwelling among them and walk among them, and I will be their God, and they shall be my people. Therefore go out from their midst, and be separate from them, says the Lord, and touch no unclean thing; then I will welcome you, and I will be a father to you, and you shall be sons and daughters to me, says the Lord Almighty"* (vv. 16-18).

If you desire to enjoy the Lord as your inheritance (Psalm 16:5-6), then the way before you is clear (v. 4). A move toward him is a step away from them, as surely as a step north means a step away from south.

The world has set its direction. They *run after another god* (v. 4). The root of the Hebrew verb is debated. Some see it as "to run" or "to chase." Others connect it to a different verb, meaning "to pay a bride price." In the latter case, it would describe the price paid for *another god.* The evidence on both sides brings no closure to the debate.

Could I venture a simple observation that remains before us, whichever root word we may assign to this verb? To go after *another god* is going to cost you something. To be sure, that is not why someone sets out after *another god*. People do so because they think it will *pay,* that the god will give them something they are seeking, something they haven't found anywhere else. They think that in this new god they have found the genie

You can't have both the Lord and this other god.

in the bottle, and in it they have a better inheritance. The sad secret that is only discovered too late is that you'll pay much more than you intended and receive far less than you hoped.

In purely physical terms, to *run after* something costs you. It costs you physical energy, to be sure (a fact that becomes increasingly obvious as I age). But more to the point, it will cost you whatever you leave behind when you set out after this other god. You can't have both, notwithstanding the whispered lies to your conscience to the contrary. To travel to one place requires leaving the place you're already in. You can't have both the Lord and this other god.

Those who set out after *another god* find that they've thrown the pearl of great price into the depths of the sea because some shard of a lovely shell has appeared on the beach. But when you dig it out from the sand, you find it is broken, partial, and a lie. You've discovered a treasure buried in a field, but instead of selling everything to purchase that field, while traveling to visit the landowner you wander off after some mirage that appeared to you on the way. In time, you discover that you have, in fact, bought a truckload of *sorrows.*

Indeed, David assures us, those sorrows *shall multiply.* You awakened too late to the jarring reality that in chasing another god you've bought a boatload of *sorrows.* You have not simply sold out to another god; you have also traded your previous life for a warehouse of *sorrows.* And not just *sorrows,* but multiplied *sorrows!* The drastic price you've paid just keeps compounding and growing day after day for the rest of your life, indeed, throughout eternity.

We are counseled to prepare early for what may be years of retirement. The bait dangled before us is the power of compounding interest. The old lure is the question, Would you rather have $1 million today or one penny today and then double your pennies each day for the next thirty days? On the face of it, the answer seems clear. Grab the million! But a moment of thought (and a bit of math) makes you realize that with the second option, you would finish the month with $10,737,418.24.

The math, however, works in the opposite direction as well, not only for gain, but also for loss. After the parents of our human race chased after *another god,* the Lord announced to them the compounding nature of the losses they had chosen. To the woman he announced, *"I will surely multiply your pain in childbearing"* (Genesis 3:16). The multiplication would continually compound the consequences for the whole race, male and female alike (vv. 16-19).

Running *after another god* compounds your sorrows

day after day, until you find yourself with more sorrows than you can carry.

It was in view of this reality that David declared, *Their drink offerings of blood I will not pour out or take their names on my lips.* I will not participate in any way in the chasing after deceitful promises and false gods, even to the speaking of their names.[30]

Do the math. Calculate the costs. Make your decision. Mine has been made.

Let me be clear. None of this makes living in calm confidence *easy,* for surely it is not. But it does make it *possible.* And the possible becomes actual through the power and grace extended to us in David's greater Son, Jesus Christ, our sweet inheritance in life and death, in time and eternity (vv. 5-6).

"The worth and excellency of a soul is to be measured by the object of its love. He who loveth mean and sordid things doth thereby become base and vile, but a noble and well-placed affection doth advance and improve the spirit into a conformity with the perfections which it loves."[31]

---

30   Cf. Exodus 23:13; Joshua 23:7.

31   Henry Scougal, *The Life of God in the Soul of Man* (Grand Rapids: Christian Ethereal Classics Library, n.d.), 13.

Chapter 8

SUFFICIENCY

*I bless the LORD who gives me counsel; in
the night also my heart instructs me.* (v. 7)

Turning from the assured scarcity of running after
another god (v. 4), we step into the sufficiency of
life with the Lord (v. 7).

There is blessing in David's heart and upon his lips.
It is directed to *the LORD who gives me counsel*. The
word rendered *counsel* designates a purpose, determination, choice, or plan. It often designates counsel given
to kings or strategies developed among them. It also
refers to the counsel or advice that upholds and guides
us to cooperate with such choices, plans, and purposes.

Above all earthly plans, there stands *the counsel of
the LORD*. It endures forever. He receives *counsel* from

no one (Isaiah 40:13-14). *The L*ORD *brings the counsel of the nations to nothing; he frustrates the plans of the peoples. The counsel of the L*ORD *stands forever, the plans of his heart to all generations* (Psalm 33:10-11). Indeed, *many are the plans in a man's heart, but the counsel of the L*ORD *will stand* (Proverbs 19:21 NASB).

Wisdom is found when I conclude that there is a will higher than mine, and when I discover that my well-being depends upon conforming to that will. At that point, I become willing to hear and heed *counsel* from the Lord, for it is a life-saving, life-giving matter.

> *"I am God, and there is no other; I am God, and there is none like me, declaring the end from the beginning and from ancient times things not yet done, saying, 'My counsel shall stand, and I will accomplish all my purpose,' calling a bird of prey from the east, the man of my counsel from a far country. I have spoken, and I will bring it to pass; I have purposed, and I will do it."*
> (Isaiah 46:9-11)

Where did David come by this *counsel* of the Lord?

In the Scriptures.

He did not have the complete revelation that we have in our Bible, which is composed of both the Old and New Testaments. But he did have some portion of it. He knew that it was in its lines that the *counsel* of the Lord could be found. The Psalms, David's great contribution to the Canon, open by declaring as much.

Blessed is the man who walks not in the counsel of the wicked, nor stands in the way of sinners, nor sits in the seat of scoffers; but his delight is in the law of the LORD, and on his law he meditates day and night (Psalm 1:1-2). And they continue to affirm this: *Your testimonies are my delight; they are my counselors* (Psalm 119:24).

David clung to God's assured promise that *I will instruct you and teach you in the way you should go; I will counsel you with my eye upon you* (Psalm 32:8). And he was not disappointed, for *"David . . . served the purpose of God in his own generation"* (Acts 13:36).

You too will find God's promise true and him faithful to it. Like Asaph, you can rest assured, *you guide me with your counsel, and afterward you will receive me to glory* (Psalm 73:24).

Jesus, the Christ, fulfilled the prophecy of Isaiah, being designated the *Wonderful Counselor* (Isaiah 9:6). For *the Spirit of the LORD . . . rest[ed] upon him, the Spirit of wisdom and understanding, the Spirit of counsel and might, the Spirit of knowledge and the fear of the LORD* (Isaiah 11:2). Jesus fulfilled God's old covenant prophecies and promises. He sent *the Spirit of counsel* to guide the authors of the New Testament.[32]

Do you understand what this means? We sit in the privileged position of having come into possession of the fullness of divine *counsel* in the pages of the Bible, both the Old and New Testaments. And *the Spirit of counsel* lives within us to teach us from its pages. How much more are we able to cry, *The LORD of hosts;*

---

32   2 Timothy 3:16; 2 Peter 1:21.

he is wonderful in counsel and excellent in wisdom (Isaiah 28:29)!

Possessing thus the counsel of the Lord, David could testify, *In the night also my heart instructs me.* But just what kind of experience is David claiming?

As perhaps you can testify, the night can be long for the troubled heart. It becomes a time when sleep flees and questions grow in one's heart.[33] At such times, the faithful have often taken up a *song in the night* which serves to help them meditate on the truth.[34] *I remember your name in the night, O LORD, and keep your law* (Psalm 119:55). *My soul yearns for you in the night; my spirit within me earnestly seeks you. For when your judgments are in the earth, the inhabitants of the world learn righteousness* (Isaiah 26:9).

This has guided me in how to harness those moments as I lay awake at night, before drifting off to sleep, or those onerous times I awaken in the night and my mind takes flight to soar over unhelpful landscapes of worry or conflict. In such moments, I need to exercise discipline of thought so the Holy Spirit can take the written Word of God I have treasured up in my heart and bring it back to me so I can reflect upon it, meditate upon it, and think it through in the quiet hours of the night.

This is usually a battle, at least for me. My thoughts, often before I realize I'm even thinking them, have taken off down the road, chasing some trouble. By the time I'm aware of their defection, I'm already behind in the battle. But through great effort, empowered by God's

---

33   Psalm 77:2; Lamentations 1:2; 2:19.
34   Psalm 77:6; cf. Isaiah 30:29.

grace, I labor to turn my thoughts to truth. When I do, God sees to it that *my heart instructs me.*

I've found that these nighttime battles can be lost before they even begin. If I do not cultivate in the daylight hours the discipline and delight of taking in God's Word, the skirmishes of the night are forfeited. I must resupply in the light so that in the night I can recall the Word.

Do you have a plan for a daily, systematic intake of God's Word? If you don't, you probably won't. And still the nights will come, and with them those long watches when the pressures and pains of the day invade and steal your peace and your sleep.

Perhaps a personal testimony will help. Some years ago, I went through a protracted season of great difficulty. I won't divulge the details, but I can assure you that it was a long season, marked by some deep bouts of depression. There were countless nights when sleep evaded me, worry invaded me,

> *Do you have a plan for a daily, systematic intake of God's Word?*

and I lay in bed staring into the darkness as I called on God. At times, my hand was stretched out to heaven, matching the pleadings of my heart.[35] Many times, tears streaked down my face and moistened my pillow.[36] I share this not because my experience is unique, but because I know it is not.

Because sleep so consistently evaded me at night, my days became more difficult. I needed rest. I realized I

---

35   Psalm 77:2.

36   Psalm 6:6; 42:3.

would only find it if I could control my thoughts when I lay down at night. I decided to memorize a psalm and use that as a means to several ends. First, I hoped it would serve to both control my thoughts and focus them on the truth. Second, the psalm itself would give form to my night-praying, which often became rambling and filled with complaint. Finally, I hoped that this would slow my whirling, out-of-control thoughts, bring a measure of calm to my heart, and allow sleep to overtake me.

Good plan, I must say. Not effortless to execute, but worth the struggle. I have found that, with discipline, all three goals are met. Not without struggle. Not without some failure along the way. But consistently, blessedly.

Psalm 16 is one of those psalms. It's been my night-companion for many years now. Through it, I can confess with David, *In the night also my heart instructs me.* These pages, I hope, are testimony to that experience.

BIRTHRIGHT AND BEAUTY

The Lord is my chosen portion and my cup; you hold my lot. The lines have fallen for me in pleasant places; indeed, I have a beautiful inheritance. (vv. 5-6)

At last, we come to the sweet center of the psalm. Here the axes of the two ends of the psalm meet and crystalize for us the beauty of our birthright as God's people through Christ. The truths on both sides of the center have shepherded us to this place where we gaze upon the Lord himself, pondering the wonder that he is his own best gift to us.

The Lord gives himself to me. The Lord chooses my portion. He gives me the highest and the best – himself in an ever-growing, deepening relationship. The Lord measures out my portion, and it includes *every spiritual blessing in the heavenly places in Christ* (Ephesians 1:3 NASB). The Lord holds my portion *imperishable and undefiled,* making certain it *will not fade away,* and keeping it *reserved in heaven for* me (1 Peter 1:4 NASB).

In view of such grace, one can only cry, *The lines have fallen for me in pleasant places; indeed, I have a beautiful inheritance* (Psalm 16:6).

> "In almost every case the beginning of new blessing is a new revelation of the character of God—more beautiful, more wonderful, more precious."[37]
> —J. Elder Cumming

> How sweet all at once it was for me to be rid of those fruitless joys which I had once feared to lose! … You drove them from me. You who are the true, sovereign joy. You drove them from me and took their place, You who are sweeter than all pleasure, though not to flesh and blood, You who outshine all light, yet are hidden deeper than any secret in our hearts, You who surpass all honor, though not in the eyes of men who see all honor in themselves. … O Lord my God, my Light, my Wealth, and my Salvation.[38]
> —Augustine

---

37   J. Elder Cumming, *Keswick Week 1906* (London: Marshalls, 1906), 22.

38   Augustine, quoted in William Varner, *Awake O Harp: A Devotional Commentary on the Psalms* (The Woodlands: Kress Biblical Resources, 2011), 45.

Chapter 9

THE LORD IS THE SELECTOR OF MY INHERITANCE

The LORD is my chosen portion. (v. 5)

Yahweh himself *is my chosen portion.* By some amazing grace, I stand in contrast to the *men of the world whose portion is in this life* (Psalm 17:14). I have him now; I shall always have him, even more fully, forever.

God promised the Israelites the land of Canaan. When they conquered it under Joshua, they then apportioned it by tribe, clan, and family. One's *portion* of land was the physical symbol of what it meant to be in covenant with God. The Levites and priests, however, did not receive an inheritance of land: *The LORD said to Aaron, "You shall have no inheritance in their land, neither shall you have any portion among them."* He promised that, instead of a physical plot of land, *"I am your portion and your inheritance among the people of Israel"* (Numbers 18:20).

This spiritual inheritance grows into a theme that runs throughout Scripture, widening from only the priests and Levites to engulf all of God's people. Thus, we read here that the Lord himself is the inheritance of his people.

Then, too, when God's people came to offer sacrifice and offerings to the Lord, the priests and Levites were given the choicest *portion* of the animal that was sacrificed. They received the choice cuts of meat.

On this side of the cross and the empty tomb, all God's people are priests to God (1 Peter 2:5, 9), and as such, our *portion* is God.

The *men of the world whose portion is in this life* cannot comprehend the misery of their position. Could there be a sadder descriptor of one's lot in life? What do they get for their living, laboring, sweating, and dying? Perhaps a small plot of land. Maybe four walls. A spouse? Children? That's great. But do they share the life that outlives this life? Or are they centered around accumulating more to stuff within their four walls? What tiny, terrestrial goals do they chase? For what inconsequential matters do they lay their lives down? When *this life* is over, they have all they will ever receive. And in that same instant, they will lose it all as they step beyond this earthly reality.

Even the highly religious, who perform their sacred deeds to be seen by others, will in the end hear only, *"Truly, I say to you, [you] have received [your] reward"* (Matthew 6:2, 5, 16). They face an empty eternity. To the one who complained of what appeared to be the inequity of his blessedness in earthly life and the emptiness of his eternal experience, the Lord answered simply, *"Remember that you in your lifetime received your good things, . . . but now . . . you are in anguish"* (Luke 16:25).

To his own, however, the Lord declares their portion is not to be found in this life. It is not found in God's gifts. Their portion is God himself. "The gift and the giver are one and the same."[39] And in giving us himself, God has given us the best he could give. He could give us stuff, money, fame, or power and position. And sometimes he does. When he does, he measures *Do we desire the Lord himself?* it out to us so we can advance his kingdom, mission, and glory. But the one thing Jesus does not hold back from us ever, but gives indiscriminately and lavishly, is himself!

All the stuff, money, position, power, and fame may be taken from us in a moment. But he will never withdraw the gift of himself. He will never slacken the flow of his divine life and fellowship with us.

The important question is what we truly want out of walking with God.

Do we desire the Lord himself? Or do we desire him merely for what he is supposed to *do* for us? Or *give* to us? Or *provide* for us?

---

39   Keil, C. F., and F. Delitzsch, *Psalms, Commentary on the Old Testament in Ten Volumes,* 5:227.

That explains *portion*, but what about *chosen*? Whom, may I ask, does the choosing? The sons of Korah answered the question definitively: *He chose our heritage for us* (Psalm 47:4). The Lord as our *chosen portion* is not a *self*-chosen inheritance, but our *divinely* chosen inheritance. It is not that we choose the Lord, but that he chose himself for us.

> "A wiser mind than our own arranges our destiny. God ordains all things, and we are glad to have it so. We choose for God to choose for us. If we could have our own way, we would want to let all things go in God's way . . . . It is my freest choice to let Him choose. As a free agent, I want Him to have absolute control."[40]

Never does the Lord fail to give to us, and to give us what is most precious and what is most necessary. If it appears God is withholding from you, you have mistaken what is going on. If he withholds one thing, it is so he can give you more of himself. But God is never a nongiver. If he withholds from you something that you desire or believe yourself in need of, look not at the hand that appears to be withholding, but at the other hand in which he is holding forth himself. He may withhold some things at times, but only so that, in all things and at all times, we may have more of him.

One day Jesus came to the home of his friends Martha and Mary. Martha busied herself with the

40   C. H. Spurgeon, *Faith's Checkbook: Daily Devotional* (updated edition, Aneko Press, 2020), entry for April 14, 112.

preparations necessary to host Jesus and his disciples (Luke 10:38, 40). Mary took her place at Jesus' feet to listen to and take in his teaching and his presence (v. 39). Martha complained to the Lord and asked him to tell her sister to get up and help (v. 40). Jesus answered her tenderly, but strongly, doubling up her name in a sign of tenderness: *"Martha, Martha, you are anxious and troubled about many things"* (v. 41). Jesus here sets up a contrast between the *many things* upon which Martha had fixed her concern and attention and the *one thing* Mary had chosen (v. 42). Concentrating on *many things* breeds and feeds anxiety and trouble. But Jesus told her, *"One thing is necessary"* (v. 42). A life of singular focus, of selective concerns, and of a singular allegiance yields something better: *"Mary has chosen the good portion, which will not be taken away from her"* (v. 42).

The Greek word translated here as *portion* is the same one used in the ancient Greek translation of Psalm 16:5 for *portion*.[41] Mary has *chosen* the good *portion* as precious to her and worthy of priority over the *many things* that could otherwise distract her.

So, yes, of course, the Lord must first choose to offer himself to us as our inheritance. He is our treasure, and it is all his doing. But it is also upon us, in worshipful response, to value what he holds forth to us. Do we value what he values supremely – himself? Do we value him as our highest treasure? Like a treasure hidden in the field for which the loss of all things yields the greatest boon possible (Matthew 13:44)? Like a pearl of great

---

41   *portion* = μερίς (*meris*).

price, for which the liquidating of all things to obtain it is the essence of wisdom (vv. 45-46)?

If we do, we will, from among the *many things* of this world that clammer for our attention, like Mary, choose the *one thing [that] is necessary, the good portion* in every event and moment of life – the Lord himself.

Chapter 10

THE LORD IS THE CONTENT OF MY INHERITANCE

The Lord is . . . my cup. (v. 5)

The Bible frequently depicts the workings of God by using the imagery of a *cup*. Of course, the Hebrew and Greek words rendered *cup* are often used literally.[42] But when used figuratively, "the cup is imagined to be filled with an experience that someone is to undergo."[43] Metaphorically, "the cup is a symbol of one's destiny. It represents one's portion in life."[44]

---

42   E.g., Genesis 40:11; Luke 22:17.

43   Lawrence O. Richards, *New International Encyclopedia of Bible Words: Based on the NIV and the NASB, Zondervan's Understand the Bible Reference Series* (Grand Rapids: Zondervan Publishing House, 1999), 206.

44   Ross, *A Commentary on the Psalms, Volume 1 (1-41)*, 405.

Often, the Bible's figurative use of *cup* points to something negative, like judgment, wrath, or suffering. The cup of God's wrath is a terrifying prospect. *Let him rain coals on the wicked; fire and sulfur and a scorching wind shall be the portion of their cup* (Psalm 11:6). *For in the hand of the LORD there is a cup with foaming wine, well mixed, and he pours out from it, and all the wicked of the earth shall drain it down to the dregs* (Psalm 75:8). *Wake yourself, wake yourself, stand up, O Jerusalem, you who have drunk from the hand of the LORD the cup of his wrath, who have drunk to the dregs the bowl, the cup of staggering* (Isaiah 51:17). On the last day, Jesus will come again *to make [Babylon] drain the cup of the wine of the fury of his wrath* (Revelation 16:19).

> *This cup of judgment is reserved for the nations who do not know or honor God.*

This cup of judgment is reserved for the nations who do not know or honor God, and even for Israel and Judah, who should have known him.[45] Indeed, all those outside God's redemption are poised, because of their sins, to drink the cup of God's wrath.[46]

Take a deep breath, pause, and let yourself consider this question: "Does that include me?"

The Bible, in contrast, speaks also of *the cup of salvation* (Psalm 116:13). This *cup* was set apart by the Father, filled by the Son, and is served to us by the Holy Spirit. It comes to us at a steep price. The Father sent his Son into the world to make provision for this *cup*. The Son

---

45 The nations: Jeremiah 25:13, 17; Israel and Judah: Isaiah 51:17, 22.

46 Psalm 75:8; Romans 6:23.

had to drink the "cup of judgment" that was due to us, draining it himself rather than having it served eternally to us. Jesus, in Gethsemane, prayed, *"My Father, if it be possible, let this cup pass from me; nevertheless, not as I will, but as you will"* (Matthew 26:39). Yet Jesus, while hanging on Golgotha the next day, drank it down, all of it, as the wrath of God for my sins and yours fell upon him.

The difference between eternally drinking the cup of God's wrath and everlastingly enjoying the cup of his salvation is Jesus. Because Jesus drank the cup of wrath that was justly ours, we may enjoy the cup of blessing and thanksgiving he offers us as a gift of grace. Through Jesus, we exclaim, as did David, *My cup overflows* (Psalm 23:5)! Through Jesus, we *lift up the cup of salvation and call on the name of the* LORD (Psalm 116:13). The night before his death, knowing what the coming hours would bring, Jesus served his disciples at that table in the upper room, explaining, *"This cup is the new covenant in my blood"* (1 Corinthians 11:25). All this favor, life, grace, and salvation comes to us out of the hand of the Lord himself.

John reports, *Then Jesus, knowing all that would happen to him, came forward* to meet not just the arresting mob, but also *the cup* of suffering and death they would deliver to him (John 18:4). When Peter drew his sword to protect Jesus, Jesus rebuked him, saying, *"Put your sword into its sheath; shall I not drink the cup that the Father has given me?"* (John 18:11). Jesus knew all that the coming hours held for him (trials, beatings, crucifixion, shame, abandonment, and death), yet he *came forward* to take that *cup* in hand and drink it to the dregs. Such courage! And the key was that he *knew* – not only *all that would happen,* but also *the cup that the Father [had] given* him. Because it was from the Father, Jesus rose to meet it. He rose and drank it so I would not have to.

In so doing, Jesus became *my cup.* When David prayed, *The* Lord . . . *is my cup,* he was not simply saying *my cup* is something given to him by the Lord. He was declaring that the Lord himself is *my cup.* Ultimately, *my cup* is not something God gives, but something God is. The blessing of God and all that constitutes his salvation comes to me via a person, by means of a relationship with that person. Jesus is both the vehicle and essence of all that God has for me. Because Jesus drank the cup of suffering, judgment, wrath, and death on my behalf, he has become the cup of God's blessing, grace, and salvation for me.

Chapter 11

THE LORD IS THE MEASURE OF MY INHERITANCE

The Lord is . . . my cup. (v. 5)

Yes, Jesus is *the Lord* who is, by his own grace, *my cup.* This is personal, relational, and intimate. Yes, and amen! But this implies still more.

When someone hands you a cup of coffee, it has dimension, size, and capacity. Standing in line at your favorite coffee shop, you may have a choice of sizes when you order your favorite hot beverage. But you don't have the option to exceed the size and capacity of the cup you select. If you order a small, you won't receive the same amount of coffee as if you had ordered a large. There is a built-in volume, limit, and capacity to every cup.

But when *the LORD is . . . my cup,* what is the capacity, volume, and limit of what I receive in him?

There's a great deal more in *a cup of cold water* than just the slacking of one's thirst (Matthew 10:42). Jesus offered *living water* to an outcast, thirsty woman he met at a well. The ensuing conversation initially confused the woman. Her understanding was limited by the physical circumstances, the absence of a container to draw up the water, and the depth of the well. But Jesus took her beyond the limited dimensions of the physical realities she had associated with water, saying, *"Whoever drinks of the water that I will give him will never be thirsty again. The water that I will give him will become in him a spring of water welling up to eternal life"* (John 4:14).

> *There's a great deal more in a cup of cold water than just the slacking of one's thirst.*

Jesus is offering her and us that which has the capacity to satisfy not just physical thirst, but also something deeper within us. He offers that which will not just meet the need of the moment, but will also render us *"never . . . again"* thirsty. Indeed, what Jesus offers us in the *cup* which he holds out to us is limitless, even *eternal.*

> *On the last day of the feast, the great day, Jesus stood up and cried out, "If anyone thirsts, let him come to me and drink. Whoever believes in me, as the Scripture has said, 'Out of his heart will flow rivers*

*of living water.'" Now this he said about
the Spirit, whom those who believed in him
were to receive, for as yet the Spirit had not
been given, because Jesus was not yet glorified.* (John 7:37-39)

The expression *living water,* found throughout the
Bible,[47] refers to flowing water as opposed to the water
in a stagnant pool. It is *living* in that it is flowing, it is
continuous, and it does not end.

Jesus measures out to us that which has no dimension, no capacity, no limit, and no measure. The Spirit
is a full member of the Trinity, sharing with the Father
and Son all the infinite dimensions of deity. The divine,
infinite Spirit applies the redemption planned by the
Father and secured by the Son when he drank fully the
cup of divine wrath due to us. He works so that the limited capacities of our human hearts are exploded by the
gifted presence of his own infinite presence and grace.

Thus, *my cup* is the Lord himself. He is not only the
vehicle and essence of what I receive from him, but he
is also the measure of all God has for me. He offers
himself to me. His being infinite means there is no end
to the grace he will pour into me. My circumstances
do not limit what God is capable of being in me, to me,
and through me. My IQ, my experiences, my personal-
ity, my physical makeup, my education, my family of
origin, my sins, my current earthly situation – none
of it! – imposes limits on what God is able and willing
to be in me, to me, and through me.

---

47   E.g., Song of Solomon 4:15; Jeremiah 17:13; Revelation 7:17.

That does not mean you should stop short of fully acknowledging and carefully considering these realities, confining and defining as they too often are. The Bible does not teach avoidance, but faith. No, look them all full in the face. Take their measure. Consider them deeply. They came to you by the Lord's own sovereign hand. Then, as you sit prayerfully in his presence, ask yourself, Have these been permitted to me for the express purpose that, through them, I might come to know the Lord more deeply and fully? Are these confining realities his invitation to rise and meet him right here, in the midst of them?

All of this confronted me as my wife and I were stepping away from thirty-three years of pastoral ministry in the United States. What was set before us was the open door to begin over again in pastoral ministry in northern Iraq. Let that sink in. The magnitude of the changes felt enormous. To be honest, the *fit* didn't feel perfect. I had questions! And we had few answers.

As we prayed through our questions, I wrote the following in my journal one day:

> "Lord Jesus, thank you for drinking the
> cup fully for me so I can know you, your
> Father, and the Spirit, and drink deeply
> of your grace. You hold my lot. Guide me,
> Jesus, please. Amen."

> So having only a tiny (but ominous) bit of
> knowledge about what leaving the USA
> and going to pastor a church in northern

Iraq would mean, I had to ask, Is this being
set before me as the *cup* by which I get to
know the Lord more deeply and fully? Is
this my invitation to rise and meet him
in this? If it is, what else would I do? He
is life! He *is my cup.* He holds *my lot.* Do I
trust him?

We rose and followed him. And oh, what a ride it has
been!

Can you honestly, with David, affirm, *The* LORD *is
. . . my cup*? Do you want him enough to allow him
to explode the limiting capacities of your life from
the inside out (*"Out of his heart,"* John 7:38), and to
pour into and through you the limitless supply of his
grace as you take him day by day as the cup the Father
hands to you?

Chapter 12

THE LORD IS THE KEEPER
OF MY INHERITANCE

Lord . . . you hold my lot. (v. 5)

The *lot* was used to determine issues that were beyond human ability to decide. Though it was not precisely the same, picture the rolling of dice. One's *lot* was what came from such a determination. The Lord is sovereign, even over what seems random to us: *The lot is cast into the lap, but its every decision is from the Lord* (Proverbs 16:33). This is how the pagan sailors discerned that their storm-tossed predicament was Jonah's fault (Jonah 1:7). It is how Zechariah came to be in the temple at the precise time the angel would appear to him and inform him of the coming miracle of his son, John (Luke 1:9). It is how the eleven remaining disciples of Jesus determined who should fill Judas's spot in their ranks (Acts 1:26).

It is not surprising, then, to learn that the *lot* is how the promised land was divided up among the tribes, clans, and families of Israel.[48] Not only was the *lot* the means for determining one's inheritance, but the word also stood for that which one received in inheritance. You may have heard someone speak of their *lot in life*.[49] It describes how circumstances have fallen out for them, what is allotted to them.

Thus, when the land was divided among the tribes and people of Israel, they had confidence that what they received came from the hand of the Lord himself. "Each Israelite could thus be sure that his portion had come from Yahweh (Proverbs 16:33). This gave a solid juridical basis for the ownership of land and must have given a sense of belonging and identity to each of the tribes and their respective families. God himself had directed what part was to be theirs."[50]

This is important for how we understand David's prayer: *LORD . . . you hold my lot.*

The verb *hold* describes both clutching something firmly and ordering events rightly. Its root describes grasping something securely.[51] The psalmist says to

---

48   Numbers 26:55-56; Joshua 14:2.
49   Cf. Ecclesiastes 3:22; 5:18-19.
50   William A. VanGemeren, ed., *New International Dictionary of Old Testament Theology and Exegesis* (Grand Rapids: Zondervan, 1997), 1:840-842.
51   Brown, Driver, and Briggs, *A Hebrew and English Lexicon of the Old Testament*, 1069.

the Lord, "[You] take and cast [the lot] for me."[52] The Lord is sovereign over the lot, when and how it is cast, what results come from its use, and how those results abide with the one who thus gains his inheritance. "The verb is also used of God's sovereign ordering of the affairs of history."[53]

As we have seen, this psalm was fulfilled in the Messiah, Jesus. It was with this utter confidence in the Father's grip on his lot – earthly and heavenly – that Jesus was able to say, *"See, the hour is at hand, and the Son of Man is betrayed into the hands of sinners"* (Matthew 26:45). No matter how dark things got, Jesus knew the hand of the Father is greater than *the hands of sinners.* Even while in the grip of his perse-cutors, Jesus could confidently declare, *"From now on you will see the Son of Man seated at the right hand of Power"* (Matthew 26:64). At the very point of death, Jesus called out with his final breath, *"Father, into your hands I commit my spirit!"* (Luke 23:46).

It is as we live in union with Jesus that we come into such confidence.

It is as we live in union with Jesus that we come into such confidence. God himself has determined that what he gives me is the highest and best possible – himself. Furthermore, he holds me securely in that position of relationship to himself. The Lord holds me securely to himself for eternity.

But even this does not exhaust the point being made here. God *holds* how I experience him along the path of

---

52   Ibid.
53   Ibid.

life. The circumstances and experiences by which the Lord gives himself to me are straight from his hand – both the positive and what I would deem as negative. Out of his own hand, the Lord gives himself to me day by day, hour by hour, moment by moment.

In New Testament terms, this speaks of our *security*. Jesus said, *"I give them eternal life, and they will never perish, and no one will snatch them out of my hand"* (John 10:28). It also speaks of the *providential rule* of my life circumstances. We do stand under that great promise: *God causes all things to work together for good to those who love God, to those who are called according to His purpose* (Romans 8:28 NASB).

The Bible's list of things God holds in his hands is long. It includes judgment (Deuteronomy 32:41) or the withholding of it (Psalm 74:11), the one who walks with him (Psalm 37:24), the thirsty one (Psalm 63:1), his people (Isaiah 41:10), and even Peter when he began to sink in the waves (Matthew 14:31). Jesus holds the churches and all related to them in his hand (Revelation 1:20; 2:1). But most amazing of all is the repeated note that he holds firmly in his hand me and all that relates to me. Should I go through a crisis of faith and awaken from it, I will discover that in all my distress, he had me by *my right hand* the whole time (Psalm 73:23; cf. Isaiah 41:13). No matter where I might find myself at any given moment in the broad expanse of God's created reality, *even there your hand shall lead me, and your right hand shall hold me* (Psalm 139:10).

This is ours because the Lord himself came down to seek us and, with nail-pierced hands, he laid hold of us for eternity.[54] There, stunned again by the magnitude of divine grace, we *humble [ourselves], therefore, under the mighty hand of God so that at the proper time he may exalt [us]* (1 Peter 5:6).

---

54   Psalm 22:16; John 20:25.

Chapter 13

THE LORD IS THE BEAUTY
OF MY INHERITANCE

*The lines have fallen for me in pleasant
places; indeed, I have a beautiful inheritance.* (v. 6)

W hen David speaks of *the lines,* he is speaking
metaphorically of the length of the cord typi-
cally used to measure out one's inheritance of land.
Picture the surveyor and the rodman with their transit
and pole, sighting in, taking readings, and recording
notations. They are precise, exact, and official.

You've been called into the attorney's office for the
reading of the will. Your loved one has left you land

– land you have never seen. You hear the cold descriptors of your tract read aloud, but they mean little to you.

You set out, excited to travel to the point on the map where you've been told you can find your inheritance. What will it be? Swampland? Desert? A fertile Eden? A mountain with a tumbling stream? A meadow filled with wildflowers under sunny skies? You crest over a hill; you stop the car. You get out and stand on a rise. There it is.

In wonder, you exclaim, *The lines have fallen for me in pleasant places*! You fall silent in awe. Then, in your hushed amazement, you hear yourself whisper, *I have a beautiful inheritance*!

The landscape the words paint is breathtaking. Metaphor is powerful, but what is the reality to which the word picture so evocatively points? The Lord himself as my inheritance. Only grace could make this so. And it has. I can say from the depths of my being (and will for eternity), *The lines have fallen for me in pleasant places; indeed, I have a beautiful inheritance.*

Life, however, is seldom so neat; our assessment of things is rarely so sanctified and satisfied. Sometimes it seems that the way circumstances *have fallen* to us is less than ideal, and perhaps even painful. Maybe you even question how a loving God could portion out this *lot* for you. What if we simply can't join David in affixing the label *pleasant* or *beautiful* to our *lot* in life?

I get it because I've lived it. Believe me.

But my mind goes to two episodes in the life of Jesus. Twice the Father interrupted the earthly events of his Son and proclaimed him as *"my beloved Son, with whom I am well pleased."* Once it was spoken to Jesus and for his personal benefit (Matthew 3:17), and once to those around him and for their benefit (Matthew 17:5). It helps me to remember that when I join David in exclaiming over my *inheritance* that it is *pleasant,* I am joining God in his good pleasure over his Son. Circumstantially, I am assured that God sovereignly directs the details of my life to maximize my experience of his Son. And yes, that, more than I care for, involves humanly unpleasant situations.

Let me also share something from my journey in the hope that there will be something helpful to you in yours. I haven't arrived, but here's some of the Lord's counsel (Psalm 16:7) that I've received along the way.

The gift and the giver are one and the same.

As I contemplate my inheritance (at least in terms of immediate circumstances), I try to remind myself that "the gift and the giver are one and the same."[55] The lines of this grace *have fallen* to me right out of God's hand and by his hand. What I am currently going through is no sign of God's abandonment. It is a sign of his love, for he is allowing this (whatever *this* may be right now) because he knows it is the quickest, surest path to giving himself more fully to me.

Also, I am learning to view this inheritance thing as not a once-for-all determination, something I'll only confess and enjoy at the end of it all. I want to view my inheritance as a daily, moment-by-moment reality, something I can enjoy every moment of every day.

---

55   Keil, C. F., and F. Delitzsch, *Psalms, Commentary on the Old Testament in Ten Volumes,* 5:227.

In the dungeon of a protracted depression, I came to a hard-earned lesson. I've come to state it in two lines. The first is this: *If Jesus is my goal, then anything can be my friend.* In this regard, the sorrows and heartbreaks of life may be better friends than the joys and pleasures. The great promise is, *God causes all things to work together for good to those who love God, to those who are called according to His purpose* (Romans 8:28 NASB). That same hope dwelt in David, for he clung to the same promise: *All the paths of the LORD are steadfast love and faithfulness, for those who keep his covenant and his testimonies* (Psalm 25:10). The bitter things speed me on my way to Jesus more quickly, undistracted by the lesser joys of this life.

Throughout the ages, those who have walked this life with calm confidence have found it to be so. While drowning in a crisis of faith, Asaph learned to confess, *My flesh and my heart may fail, but God is the strength of my heart and my portion forever* (Psalm 73:26). In the midst of a run for his life and while hiding in a cave, David declared, *I cry to you, O LORD; I say, "You are my refuge, my portion in the land of the living"* (Psalm 142:5). When his entire world had been destroyed, Jeremiah could still say, *"The LORD is my portion," says my soul, "therefore I will hope in him"* (Lamentations 3:24).

It is true, that if Jesus is my goal, then anything can become my friend. But a second line is necessary for honesty's sake: *If anything else is my goal, then everything becomes my enemy.* That's why David said, *The sorrows of those who run after another god shall multiply* (Psalm 16:4). God arrays himself in opposition against the proud and independent.[56] He who neither wastes nor withholds anything that will maximize my enjoyment of and conformity to him also deploys them against me when he sees me wandering after worthless things.

God wastes nothing to speed me toward my true goal – more of Jesus. Likewise, he is dedicated to wasting nothing in all creation to impede my way toward my tragic goal – life without him.

When I have the Lord as my inheritance, I know the Lord himself *chooses* my circumstances and my experience of him, *measures* my circumstances and my experience of him, and *holds* my circumstances and my experience of him within them. What arrangement could ever be more *pleas-ant*? What could be more *beautiful*?

God wastes nothing to speed me toward my true goal – more of Jesus.

There is yet another angle on David's two lines of exultant joy that we must consider. As we have noted throughout our preceding discussion, this is a Jesus-psalm. This psalm was ultimately fulfilled in our Savior. He is David's greater Son, for whom the words of this psalm were ultimately intended. He fulfills them. He lived them. He made them his own.

So, we should ask, What did this line sound like on Jesus' lips? Upon what was his mind set during his march toward the cross, during those hours of humiliation and suffering, and as he died? What could form in his heart a landscape of *pleasant places* amid all that? While suffering so, over what did he marvel and declare it *beautiful*?

---

56   James 4:6; 1 Peter 5:5.

In short, what was the *inheritance* of Jesus over which he marveled with delight?

We are!

Ponder that for a moment. Don't rush.

Is this possible?

Paul would pray for Jesus-followers many years later that *having the eyes of your hearts enlightened, . . . you may know what is the hope to which he has called you, what are the riches of his glorious inheritance in the saints* (Ephesians 1:18). In the Old Testament, we often read of Israel as God's inheritance.[57] Here the apostle applies the same imagery to those who are Jesus' through the New Covenant.[58] "Here we see the church and people of God, the chosen ones who are given to Christ as his portion and inheritance. The sense is that Christ's portion lies among or in the pleasant persons of his inheritance."[59]

Jesus, looking forward to the glorified state in which you and I will dwell with him and all his redeemed, declared *beautiful*! His heart counted that eternal existence with us as *pleasant places* worth dying to obtain. Even while suffering and dying, Jesus counted himself blessed to come into you, me, and all the others like us as his very own. There was a *joy that was set before him* even as he *endured the cross,* a joy so great that the anticipation of it enabled him to despise the shame of what he was enduring (Hebrews 12:2). You and I are

---

57   E.g., Deuteronomy 4:20; Psalm 33:12; Isaiah 63:17; Jeremiah 10:16.

58   Max Turner, "Ephesians," *New Bible Commentary: 21st Century Edition,* D. A. Carson, R. T. France, J. A. Motyer, G. J. Wenham, eds. (Downers Grove, Illinois: InterVarsity Press, 1994), 1227-1228.

59   John Gill, *Exposition of the Bible,* quoted in *Church History Study Bible,* Stephen J. Nichols, Gen. Ed. (Wheaton: Crossway, 2023), 772.

not the sum of that inheritance, but by his grace we are a part of it.

Simply astonishing!

Of course, the Bible clearly tells us we come into an inheritance given to us by the Father as he placed us in union with Christ.[60] While the whole of that inheritance awaits the final estate, we are already brought into the experience of it through the ministry of the Holy Spirit.[61]

Inheritance? Jesus' is found in us; ours is found in him. A reciprocal joy of eternal fellowship that can only ever be *pleasant* and *beautiful.*

What do you give to the one who already has everything, has created everything, and rules everything? Us! For eternity, to look upon the one who, at the cost of his own life, made me his own inheritance and to realize he counts the redeemed, sanctified, and ultimately glorified me as *beautiful, pleasant,* and utterly worth it only makes me cry, *"Beautiful!"* over him and count my relationship to him the most *pleasant* of all possible inheritances.

---

60 E.g., Ephesians 1:11, 14.
61 Ephesians 1:13-14.

Section 5

FELLOWSHIP DIVINE

You make known to me the path of life; in your presence there is fullness of joy; at your right hand are pleasures forevermore. (v. 11)

David's closing prayer (v. 11) does not so much add new material as it basks in the great gift at the center of this psalm – the Lord our inheritance (vv. 5-6). David is consciously, in the presence of God, taking this superlative gift of grace and looking with wonder and worship upon him. Like a diamond, polished and displayed on velvet under intense lighting, emanating from every angle, David gazes upon this privileged fellowship with God himself. Read these three lines with me again, with tones of amazement, and a whisper of wonder. Slowly tumble this gem in the surf of your ongoing thoughts.

Set before us here is a path to walk, a presence in which to dwell, and pleasures to enjoy forever.

> "When we focus our minds on God, we will love him all the more. In enjoying him we will be overwhelmed with a joy beyond what words can describe. For here on earth God is known only in part, but in heaven we shall know him more fully."[62]
> —Martin Bucer

> "The things that began to happen after that were so great and beautiful that I cannot write them. And for us this is the end of all the stories. . . . But for them it was only the beginning of the real story. All their life in this world and all their adventures in Narnia had only been the cover and title page: now at last they were beginning Chapter One of the Great Story which no one on earth has read: which goes on forever: in which every chapter is better than the one before."[63]
> —C. S. Lewis

62 Martin Bucer, *Five Books of the Sacred Psalms,* quoted in *Church History Study Bible,* Stephen J. Nichols, Gen. Ed. (Wheaton: Crossway, 2023), 773.

63 C. S. Lewis, *The Chronicles of Narnia* (New York: HarperCollins, 2005), 767.

Chapter 14

THE PATH OF THE LORD

You make known to me the path of life. (v. 11)

From the start, Christianity was designated simply as *the Way.*[64] The gospel leads those who embrace it not just to an end but also to a beginning, not just to a destination but also to a journey. Yes, of course, Jesus saved those who turned to him. But in doing so, he invited them into a journey that would bring to pass their salvation in its fullest sense. When Jesus said, *"I am the way, and the truth, and the life"* (John 14:6), he was indicating that following him in faith is a journey along which the *way,* and the *truth,* and even *life* itself will become more fully real, whole, and personal with each step we take with him.

---

64   Acts 9:2; 19:9, 23; 24:14, 22.

Little wonder, then, that the resurrected Christ's first words to the Father after exiting the grave could rightly have been these: *You make known to me the path of life* (Psalm 16:11). In his incarnation, his life of humility in the very world he created, the sufferings of his passion, and even his death (and each painful moment and detail along the way) – all of them served to *make known to [Jesus] the path of life* in the fullest possible of ways.

Wonder of wonders that you and I, as those who have entered the benefits of Jesus' passion and resurrection, can address him with the same words.

Just what are we to make of this phrase, *the path of life*? What did Jesus mean by this when he prayed this back to the Father? What should we make of it? Is this the path that *leads to* life? Is this the path that *is* life? The former would have an eye to the fullness of salvation realized on the other side of Jesus' return and the establishment of his universal reign. The latter would primarily indicate the step-by-step relationship we enjoy with him as we pass through this life and all its sundry experiences, finding along the way that, in his sovereignty and love, he makes everything *life* for us.

The answer?

Yes! Yes to both. It is life that begins now and here. It is life that is more fully ours one step at a time with Jesus through this life, as he gives us more and more of himself. It is the life of eternity that is life at its fullest, never to be diminished, diluted, or taken from us.

That makes this a prayer to offer at the opening of our journey with Jesus. It is a prayer to make our own moment by moment as we travel this earthly life with him. And it will be our glorious exclamation when we are welcomed into his presence in heaven.

Let's think a bit more about the second of those realities. Having *set the LORD always before me* (v. 8), I discover that Jesus was telling the truth when he declared, *"I am the way"* (John 14:6). He is the way to everything, not just the gate that opens on the way.[65] Yes, he is that too. But he is also the very *way*, the path, the road, the trail itself – the daily, plodding, step-by-step life of discipleship that emerges into the very *friendship of the LORD* (Psalm 25:14).

> *He is the way to everything, not just the gate that opens on the way.*

It is along that way that I come to discover that *all the paths of the LORD are steadfast love and faithfulness, for those who keep his covenant and his testimonies* (Psalm 25:10). Utilizing all the things encountered along the way, Jesus is continually unfolding life for me so that I might experience, live in, be restored by, and delight in his *steadfast love.* All the scenes that pass by me (and pass through me) as I walk with Jesus each day are his personalized curriculum on the *faithfulness* of his covenant love for me. In the flow of life's events, Jesus *makes known to [me] his covenant* (v. 14). There he makes me realize and enjoy *the friendship of the LORD* (v. 14). Precisely because he is *good and upright,* the Lord *instructs sinners in the way* (v. 8). He makes known, teaches, leads, and instructs *the humble [in] his way* (vv. 4-9).

---

65   John 10:1, 7, 9.

Behind the metaphor of *the path* is the reality of God giving us life, one moment at a time, one experience at a time, one breath at a time, and all this by the indwelling of his own Spirit. This is how God intends us to increasingly discover and live in Jesus' own resurrection life here and now. This is a life that does not end at the close of our physical, earthly voyage, but that goes on forever. Along this path, we discover life with Jesus as a never-ending journey.

Verse 11 sets this life before us under three key words. Walking this road, the Lord reveals it to me as a *path* that without fail leads me to experience and live in his *presence,* and that moves me deeper and deeper into his own *pleasures.*

Where God leads you, *how* he leads you, *what* he leads you through, and *what* he shows you along the way are meant to lead you deeper into his own life shared with you. Ironically, this is where we often have the most complaints against God and the way he is shepherding our lives. Discipleship is the painful joy of discovering that it is precisely down this path that I most deeply enter his presence and share most profoundly in his pleasures.

Could Jesus truly be *that* good? That loving? That sovereign? That powerful? That faithful? Could life with Jesus genuinely be *that* personal?

The call of the gospel is still, *"Come and see"* (John 1:46).

Chapter 15

THE PRESENCE
OF THE LORD

In your presence there is fullness of joy. (v. 11)

The Lord sovereignly directs the details of your life so that they form a pathway leading you ever further into his *presence.*

The Hebrew word rendered *presence* is literally *face.* With the accompanying preposition, it describes being in "front of."[66] The Lord is shaping your daily experiences and the broader movements of your life to shepherd you into a life of face-to-face relationship with himself. In this, he is matching your commitment to *set the Lord always before* yourself (v. 8). He is true

---

66 Brown, Driver, and Briggs, *A Hebrew and English Lexicon of the Old Testament,* 818.

to his promise: *Draw near to God, and he will draw near to you* (James 4:8).

Jesus personally leads you moment by moment, experience by experience, into a face-to-face life with himself. Don't ease past that. Pause and contemplate it. There are no wasted moments. No unused experiences. No chance happenings. All of it is portioned out to you so that you will lift your eyes and find yourself living face-to-face with Jesus.

Again, resist the whisper to take that lightly.

Jacob, out of his night of wrestling, marveled, saying, *"I have seen God face to face, and yet my life has been delivered"* (Genesis 32:30). Gideon cried out in fear, *"I have seen the angel of the LORD face to face"* (Judges 6:22). But it was Moses who would be most known for this kind of relationship with the Lord. *The LORD used to speak to Moses face to face, as a man speaks to his friend* (Exodus 33:11). The Lord himself admitted, *"With him I speak mouth to mouth"* (Numbers 12:8). And, alas, following his time, the people admitted, *There has not arisen a prophet since in Israel like Moses, whom the LORD knew face to face* (Deuteronomy 34:10).

Yet the Lord himself commanded the priests to pray over the people: *"The LORD bless you and keep you; the LORD make his face to shine upon you and be gracious to you; the LORD lift up his countenance upon you and give you peace"* (Numbers 6:24-26).

The Lord is pursuing this intimacy with each of his people – indeed, with you. If the priests were to pray this over the people of Israel, will our Great High Priest, Jesus, intend less for us who live under the *better covenant* of his blood (Hebrews 7:22)? He gave us his own Spirit so that he might be as close to us as our own breath is to our lungs.[67]

Truly, we must admit that *now we see in a mirror dimly,* but there is coming a day when it will be *face to face.* Yes, *now I know in part; [but] then I shall know fully, even as I have been fully known* (1 Corinthians 13:12). Yet don't underestimate the intimacy avail-

This kind of intimacy with God changes everything.

able to you in the present. For the Father *has sent the Spirit of his Son into our hearts, crying, "Abba! Father!"* (Galatians 4:6).

This kind of intimacy with God changes everything. The presence of the Lord gives light, awe, courage, refreshment, vindication, security, salvation, and more.[68] Here, *fullness of joy* is promised as we live in the Lord's presence.

Jesus, *for the joy that was set before him endured the cross.* With that joy before him, he scorned *the shame* of it all. It was joy over being set in the intimacy of being *at the right hand of the throne of God* that powered Jesus' endurance and sacrifice (Hebrews 12:2). Because Jesus *set the LORD always before* himself, he found the Father always *at [his] right hand.* This is why he could *not be shaken* throughout his sufferings (Psalm 16:8). In this world, Jesus was ever seeking face-to-face fellowship with the Father and, experientially, always finding him at his right hand. Now he is seated forever at the

---

67   Acts 16:7; Philippians 1:19.
68   Psalm 90:8; 114:7; 23:4; Acts 3:20; Psalm 17:2; 23:5; 31:20; 41:12.

Father's right hand, enjoying forever the intimacy of the triune God.

We are invited into this kind of fellowship![69] It is little wonder we are urged to *seek his presence continually* (Psalm 105:4). We echo Asaph's testimony: *As for me, the nearness of God is my good* (Psalm 73:28 NASB). It is face-to-face with the Lord of glory that we whisper to him, *I have no good apart from you* (Psalm 16:2).

The noun *joy* is in the plural form, to "emphasize the degree of joy experienced."[70] And notice, it is **fullness** *of joy* that is ours. The Hebrew word rendered *fullness* describes being sated or satisfied. We would say *stuffed,* as with food. The form here signifies "satisfying abundance."[71] We testify, with a chuckle of reverie, that *my cup overflows* (Psalm 23:5)!

If all this seems a bit too much, remember, this was the prayer bursting off of Jesus' lips when he left the tomb forever and stepped again into the circle of triune fellowship. Hear Jesus' promise: You *"will be loved by my Father, and I will love [you] and manifest myself to [you]"* and *"my Father will love [you], and we will come to [you] and make our home with [you]"* (John 14:21, 23).

God, whose own best inheritance-gift to us is himself, is committed to making you realize and live in the highest level of intimacy with him. If, in the short term, he doesn't make things easier, more comfortable, or according to your preferences, then know that it is so that he might give himself more fully to you. If he

---

69   John 14:18-23.

70   NET Bible.

71   Brown, Driver, and Briggs, *A Hebrew and English Lexicon of the Old Testament,* 959.

makes you wait, makes you wonder, makes you question, or makes you frustrated, it is so that you might know more of his presence. God is always in the business of giving to his children, and that which he most delights to give is himself.

Chapter 16

THE PLEASURES
OF THE LORD

*At your right hand are pleasures
forevermore.* (v. 11)

G od's goal in giving himself to you is that everything that makes up the path of your relationship
to him will lead you to live consciously and truly in
his presence moment by moment, and that in living
there you come into *pleasures* that you will share with
him *forevermore.*

This isn't the first time we have met this word *pleasures.* It is at the heart of an inheritance-gift so great
that we cried out, *The lines have fallen for me in **pleasant** places* (v. 6). But here *pleasures,* as with *joy* in the
previous line, is in the plural form, emphasizing that

these *pleasures* are multiple, innumerable, and inexhaustible. The "degree of delight experienced" knows no limit.[72]

The people of the world do not often associate pleasure with God. In fact, many of them believe him to be diametrically opposed to pleasure, like the cynic who once defined puritanism as the haunting fear that someone, somewhere, may be happy.[73]

Such folks have simply not read the Bible.

The Bible tells us God exists, *"declaring the end from the beginning, and from ancient times things which have not been done, saying, 'My purpose will be established, and I will accomplish all **My good pleasure'"*** (Isaiah 46:10 NASB).

Note those final three words: *My good pleasure.*

God created everything. God is thus sovereign over all things. God rules everything in his providence. And by *everything,* he means *everything,* from *the beginning* to *the end* and all that fills the gaps in between.

God is sovereign over all things.

Everything. Every person. Every detail. Every moment.

God, from *the beginning,* built a purpose into it all – his *good pleasure.*

There is good news and bad news in that revelation. The good news is: God isn't necessarily against pleasure, but he is against solo pleasures, selfish pleasures. That leads us to the bad news: God isn't hereby endorsing, resourcing, or empowering your self-oriented pursuit of pleasure. God is not trying to rob you of pleasure.

---

72 NET Bible.

73 H. L. Mencken, *A Mencken Chrestomathy* (New York: Alfred A. Knopf, 1949), 624.

He's working to save you from puny pleasures. In fact, God is calling you to a life (here and later) filled with greater pleasures than you can now imagine or ever gain on your own.

God wants to share his pleasures with you.

But there is still more! Are you ready for it?

Your highest pleasure is wrapped up in God's greatest pleasure.[74]

God is infinite, boundless, and limitless. So then, also, are his pleasures. God does not wish to diminish your pleasure, but to infinitely expand it!

The film *Chariots of Fire* is a dramatized account of the life of Eric Liddell, Scotland's great Olympic champion. Liddell was born in China where his parents served as missionaries. In time he was sent to England for schooling. He became convinced of God's call upon his life and planned to return to China for a lifetime of service to God. He did eventually return, and there he died, far too young, from a cancerous brain tumor. But God had not only created Eric to be a missionary; he had also given him astounding athletic abilities. A moving scene in the film depicts Eric's sister, Jenny, as she frets over all the time and attention he is giving to running. She worries that he will lose sight of God's call for him to China. Eric answers her with the immortal words, "God made me for China. But God also made me fast, and when I run, I feel his pleasure."

---

74   The remainder of this chapter is adapted from my book, *Long Story Short: God, Eternity, History, and You* (Fort Washington, PA: CLC Publications, 2010), 30-31.

God has, by his grace, created you and rules your life so that you can, devoted to his glory, share with him in his pleasure. Again, please understand, God is not against *your* pleasure. He is seeking rather to save you from merely finite, passing, and ultimately disappointing gratifications. He wants to rescue you from being far too easily satisfied with momentary, fleeting things. He wants you to enter *his pleasure* – a pleasure that is not gone as quickly as the food is swallowed, the sex is over, or the spotlight moves from you to someone else. Jesus wants to draw you into the unceasing flow of his eternal joy.

God has an inheritance-gift for you – himself – now, and more fully, forever. That shared life involves a purpose bigger than you've ever imagined. It involves gains bigger than you've ever dreamed. It involves pleasure more intense than you've ever fantasized.

See him there! Our risen Savior (v. 10), who is standing at your *right hand* (Psalm 16:8), is now established forever at the Father's *right hand.* There *forevermore,* he is enjoying *pleasures* beyond measure. It is as if he raises his ecstasy-lighted face to gaze upon you, motion you toward himself, and says, "Come! I don't want to enjoy this without you!"

Jesus is the *path* leading to the Father's *presence,* where, with him, he enjoys infinite *pleasures* forevermore. This is what he wishes to share with you.

In him, you have everything. Indeed, C. S. Lewis was correct when he said, "He who has God and everything else has no more than he who has God alone."[75]

---

75   Lewis, *The Weight of Glory and Other Addresses*, 34.

EPILOGUE

There you have it. This is my best attempt to capture in words the things God has been dealing with me about for years, and doing it through Psalm 16. My words fail to mark the trail as clearly as I would like. Nor do they adequately describe the sweetness I have found in traveling it. If nothing else, take my words as the simple, rudimentary markings of an old traveler who has passed this way before. Perhaps they amount to nothing more than a crude arrow, scrawled on the pathway with the nub of a blunt piece of sidewalk chalk. But inadequate as they are, may they point you forward and urge you on. Whatever you make of these lines, I pray that they will prod you onward to gain the prize of your inheritance, not only *in* Christ, but also *who is* Christ.

So, now it's time. You must make Psalm 16 and the realities it holds forth your own. Take your first steps by setting this book aside and opening your Bible to this psalm. Now pray it back to the Lord, who set it before you. To Jesus, pray (and keep on praying), "I am yours!" (vv. 1-4). With gratitude, affirm by faith, "You are mine!" (vv. 5-8). With your confidence resting squarely on him, declare, "Life is ours together, forever!" (vv. 9-11).

Now go. Live in calm confidence with him who is your *chosen portion, cup,* and *beautiful inheritance.*

APPENDIX

The Exposition of Psalm 16

A SINGLE MESSAGE

THE TREASURES OF GOD (VV. 1-11)

1. God's protection. (vv. 1-4)

2. God's provision. (vv. 5-8)

3. God's promise. (vv. 9-11)

or

DIVINE FELLOWSHIP (VV. 1-11)

1. Our plea and God's promise. (vv. 1, 10)

2. Our consecration and God-confidence. (vv. 2-3, 8-9)

3. Our separation and God's sufficiency. (vv. 4, 7)

4. Our birthright and God's beauty. (vv. 5-6)

5. Our prospects and God's path. (v. 11)

or

THE PRAYER OF LIFE (VV. 1-11)

1. I am yours! (vv. 1-4)

2. You are mine! (vv. 5-8)

3. Life is ours together, forever! (vv. 9-11)

A THREE-PART SERIES:
LIVING IN CALM CONFIDENCE

MESSAGE #1: THE CONFIDENCE OF GOD'S PROTECTION. (VV. 1-4)

1. The protection of God's care. (vv. 1-2)

   a. God provides preservation. (v. 1)

   b. God provides refuge. (v. 1)

   c. God procures my confession. (v. 2)

2. The protection of God's community. (vv. 3-4)

   a. I stand among God's people. (v. 3)

   b. I stand apart from God's enemies. (v. 4)

MESSAGE #2: THE CONFIDENCE
OF GOD'S PROVISION. (VV. 5-8)

1. God is my inheritance. (vv. 5-6)

2. God is my counsel. (vv. 7-8)

MESSAGE #3: THE CONFIDENCE
OF GOD'S PROMISE. (VV. 9-11)

1. God promises me joy. (v. 9)

2. God promises me life. (v. 10)

3. God promises me hope. (v. 11)

    a. God's Path leads us to . . . (v. 11)

    b. God's Presence, which yields for us . . . (v. 11)

    c. God's Pleasures. (v. 11)

A FIVE-PART SERIES:
LIVING IN CALM CONFIDENCE

MESSAGE #1: OUR PLEA AND
GOD'S PROMISE. (VV. 1, 10)

1. Our plight and plea. (v. 1)

2. Our Provider and promise (v. 10)

MESSAGE #2: OUR CONSECRATION AND
GOD-CONFIDENCE. (VV. 2-3, 8-9)

1. Our consecration. (vv. 2-3)

    a. To God. (v. 2)

    b. To God's people. (v. 3)

  2. Our confidence. (vv. 8-9)

    a. Confidence concerning our security. (v. 8)

    b. Confidence concerning our safety. (v. 9)

MESSAGE #3: OUR SEPARATION AND GOD'S SUFFICIENCY. (VV. 4, 7)

  1. Our separation. (v. 4)

  2. God's sufficiency. (v. 7)

MESSAGE #4: OUR BIRTHRIGHT AND GOD'S BEAUTY. (VV. 5-6)

  1. The Lord is the selector of my inheritance. (v. 5)

  2. The Lord is the content of my inheritance. (v. 5)

  3. The Lord is the measure of my inheritance. (v. 5)

  4. The Lord is the keeper of my inheritance. (v. 5)

  5. The Lord is the beauty of my inheritance. (v. 6)

MESSAGE #5: FELLOWSHIP DIVINE. (V. 11)

  1. The Path of the Lord. (v. 11)

  2. The Presence of the Lord. (v. 11)

  3. The Pleasures of the Lord. (v. 11)

ABOUT THE AUTHOR

John Kitchen grew up on the plains of rural Iowa as part of a good, but unbelieving family. After his sister, father, and he nearly died in an asphyxiation accident, his mother began seeking God. A few years later, his sister came to personal faith in Christ through the witness of friends. She in turn led John to Christ while he was in junior high school. Later, as a young adult, John sensed God's call to ministry and began training for his service.

John has been preaching God's Word for over forty years, having served as a pastor from the Midwest to the Middle East. John holds a doctor of ministry degree from Trinity Evangelical Divinity School, a master of divinity degree from Columbia Biblical Seminary, and a bachelor of arts degree from Crown College. He has taught God's Word in numerous countries on five continents of the world and has published more than a dozen books. You can follow John's ministry at www.jkitchen.org.

www.ingramcontent.com/pod-product-compliance
Lightning Source LLC
Chambersburg PA
CBHW071519120626
46550CB00006B/2285